Keynes and Philosophy

Keynes and Philosophy

Essays on the Origin of Keynes's Thought

Edited by
Bradley W. Bateman
Assistant Professor of Economics
Grinnell College, Iowa
and John B. Davis
Assistant Professor of Economics
Marquette University

Edward Elgar

Published by
Edward Elgar Publishing Limited
The Lypiatts
15 Lansdown Road
Cheltenham
Glos GL50 2JA
UK

Edward Elgar Publishing, Inc.
William Pratt House
9 Dewey Court
Northampton
Massachusetts 01060
USA

Paperback edition 1993
Cased edition reprinted 2015

British Library Cataloguing in Publication Data
Keynes and philosophy: essays on the origin of Keynes's
    thought.
    1. Economics. Theories of Keynes, John Maynard, 1883–1946
    I. Bateman, Bradley W. *1956–*   II. Davis, John B.
    330.156

Library of Congress Cataloguing in Publication Data
Keynes and philosophy: essays on the origin of Keynes's thought/
    [edited by] Bradley W. Bateman and John B. Davis.
        p.   cm.
    Includes bibliographical references and index.
        1. Keynes, John Maynard, 1883–1946.   2. Keynesian economics.
    I. Bateman, Bradley W., 1956–   .   II. Davis, John Bryan.
    HB103.K47K385 1991   90–46812
                                                             CIP

ISBN   978 1 85278 306 8 (cased)
           978 1 85278 845 2 (paperback)

Printed and bound in Great Britain by T.J. International Ltd, Padstow

Contents

Contributors

B. W. Bateman is an assistant professor at Grinnell College in the United States. His articles on Keynes's early work in philosophy have appeared in the *American Economic Review*, *Economics and Philosophy*, and the *History of Political Economy*.

A. Carabelli is an associate professor at Pavia University in Italy. She is the author of *On Keynes's Method* and several articles on Keynes in English and Italian.

J. B. Davis is an assistant professor at Marquette University, and is the editor of the *Review of Social Economy*. His articles on Keynes's work in philosophy and economics have appeared in the *Economic Journal*, the *Cambridge Journal of Economics*, and the *Journal of Post-Keynesian Economics*.

Athol Fitzgibbons is a lecturer at Griffith University in Australia. He is the author of *Keynes' Vision*.

Suzanne Helburn is Professor of Economics at the University of Colorado, Denver in the United States. She is the editor of *Marx, Schumpeter and Keynes: A Centenary Celebration of Dissent*.

Rod O'Donnell is a senior lecturer at Macquarie University in Australia. He is the author of *Keynes: Economics, Philosophy and Politics*.

Yuichi Shionoya is the President of Hitotsubashi University in Japan. He is the author of several books including *The Structure of Values: Utility vs. Rights*, and is the translator of Keynes's *General Theory* into Japanese.

1.   Introduction

Bradley W. Bateman and John B. Davis

It is not clear what draws so many scholars to the work of J.M. Keynes. There are certainly several possibilities: his central role in the development of modern macroeconomics; the widespread belief that he 'saved capitalism' with his advocacy of deficit spending during the Great Depression; his part at the Versailles Peace Conference and fame as the author of *The Economic Consequences of the Peace*; his activity at Bretton Woods in the founding of the post-war monetary system; his involvement in the avant-garde Bloomsbury group. But, whatever the reasons, there seems to be no decline in interest in Keynes's lifetime of work, as each year the number of essays and books published on Keynes continues to increase. Indeed, in the 1980s, interest in Keynes's work began to spread beyond the writings and discussions of economists, as historians (Clarke, Skidelsky, Peden) and political scientists (Hall, Skocpol, Hadley, Gourevitch) added their contributions to the growing literature on Keynes.

Another new area of interest has been the philosophical dimensions of Keynes's early thinking and its relationship to his later work in economics. Ironically, although most standard treatments of the history of probability theory include a discussion of Keynes's *Treatise on Probability*, until recently the existence of the *Treatise* and Keynes's early career as a philosopher have gone largely unnoticed by economists. Indeed, for many years it had been standard practice to explain *The General Theory* as the end-product of an evolution that began with *A Tract on Monetary Reform* and *A Treatise on Money*, while ignoring Keynes's earlier intellectual development in his first years at Cambridge; this despite the fact that it is in the *Treatise on Probability* that Keynes first develops ideas which were arguably later to underlie his thinking about expectations and uncertainty – an area of considerable importance in *The General Theory*.

It is fair to say that much of the new interest in Keynes's early thinking can be traced to a widespread preoccupation with expectations in modern macroeconomics in the 1970s and 1980s, and the recent recognition that Keynes's own thinking about expectations dated from his early philo-

1

sophical investigation of probability and induction in the *Treatise on Probability*. Thus, although Keynesian economic theory was, for a time, popularly considered obsolete on account of its supposed neglect of expectations, economists have increasingly come to recognize that Keynes's thinking in this regard was both extensive and well motivated by carefully considered philosophical positions in probability theory. This has drawn attention to the entire trajectory of Keynes's intellectual career and has demonstrated to many the central role of philosophical assumptions in economics.

It is important to note, however, that the *Treatise on Probability* does not mark the beginning of Keynes's work in philosophy; it is the culmination of over 15 years' work. Initial convictions for thinkers of great insight and synthetic understanding are often important to their later intellectual development, and Keynes himself testified in his 1938 'My Early Beliefs' memoir to the importance of the earliest Cambridge influences on the development of his later thinking. These influences concerned, of course, the considerable impression which the well-known Cambridge philosopher G.E. Moore's *Principia Ethica* had upon Keynes and other members of the Cambridge Conversazione Society, or Apostles. Keynes in fact wrote a number of yet unpublished philsophical papers on topics in Moore's *Principia*, a number of which (in particular, his 1904 'Ethics in Relation to Conduct') have recently been argued by scholars to have contributed to Keynes's first ideas for his *Treatise on Probability*, as well as to his later economic thinking. The interest in Keynes as a philosopher, then, is still quite fresh, and attention to Keynes's early intellectual career promises to form an important part of future scholarship on Keynes.

The essays in this collection represent an introduction to the work of a number of the people currently concerned with the philosophical foundations of Keynes's thought. Each of the essays is an original contribution that reflects the author's perspective on interpreting Keynes's philosophy.

The first essay, by Yuichi Shionoya, examines the relationship between Keynes's much-quoted 'My Early Beliefs' memoir and his philosophical beginnings at Cambridge in Moore's circle. Shionoya argues that Keynes adopted Moore's meta-ethical intuitionism and agreed that hedonism was an inadequate conception of the good, whilst rejecting Moore's consequentialist teleology and emphasis on rules in determining right behaviour. This interpretation of Keynes's early positions is distinguished from that associated with R.B. Braithwaite's influential reading of

Keynes's philosophical views and thus serves an important function in setting forth the issues first addressed by those concerned to connect the different stages of Keynes's intellectual career. Shionoya also discusses the relationship between Keynes's ethics and politics.

Indeed, some of the most vexing questions about Keynes's thinking concern his political philosophy. What spirit and ideology informed his lifelong professional interest in economic management? Suzanne Helburn finds the answer in Keynes's early interest in the work and life of Edmund Burke. Because Burke is noted for his conservative thought, this association may seem paradoxical at first, but Helburn's careful exegesis is successful in illuminating the similarities and differences between the two thinkers. She argues that the dimensions of Keynes's utilitarian analysis, ethics and élitism all stem from his understanding of this eighteenth-century political philosopher.

Bradley Bateman's essay on the analytical foundations of Keynes's policy proposals is an attempt to break with much of the emerging literature on Keynes's philosophical background. Unlike those who argue that Keynes developed one philosophical position in his youth which informs all his later thinking, Bateman uses Keynes's statements during the 1930s that his beliefs had changed to tell a much different story. On this telling, it was Keynes's shift from a belief in objective value and objective probabilities to a belief in subjective value and subjective probabilities that provided him with the tools necessary for modelling expectations and making satisfactory policy recommendations. Understanding this perspective also involves a break with the naive view that *The General Theory* is a book meant to advocate fiscal fine-tuning.

Rod O'Donnell's essay on the weight of argument in Keynes's theoretical work is an effort to clarify some of the confusion surrounding an often misunderstood idea. O'Donnell traces the origins of the concept of weight in Keynes's early work, and discusses its role in the *Treatise on Probability* and *The General Theory*. He argues that weight is not identical to evidence but, rather, that it represents the credence which a given amount of evidence provides for a probability; although credence always increases with the amount of evidence, the two notions are not identical. O'Donnell concludes by arguing that Keynes's lifelong interest in the improved collection and dissemination of economic data was partly motivated by his concern with weight.

In his essay, John Davis turns to Keynes's 1938 characterization of economics as a moral science and investigates how this view was rooted in Keynes's early philosophical convictions. Davis argues that Keynes stressed the importance of introspection and judgements of value for understanding economic agents' responses to the uncertainties of action, and did so with the intention of contrasting his view of economics to that of Lionel Robbins. For Keynes, introspection and judgements of value are made possible by individuals' capacity for both individual judgement and for judging what is intersubjectively objective. Robbins's rejection of interpersonal utility comparisons stemmed from a failure to recognize that latter dimension to human judgement; Keynes's attention to this dimension, it is suggested, underlies his view of the independent variables of *The General Theory*.

In her essay, Anna Carabelli also turns to Keynes's methodological thinking by examining the underlying principles of Keynes's critique of what he termed 'classical theory'. She argues that Keynes recognized the ineffectiveness of past critiques of orthodox theory, and that a successful critique demanded new epistemological thinking. Indeed, the fault of classical theory lay neither in its empirical unacceptability nor in logical inconsistency but rather in certain of its tacit assumptions concerning 'logical independence' which effectively defined its domain of validity in universal terms. Keynes, however, rejected these assumptions, and in turn developed an understanding of an organic interrelation among the key variables of a 'complex' economic system. Carabelli concludes that Keynes's methodological views are central to his elaboration of an alternative economic theory.

Another area of interest in Keynes's philosophical work is his early idealism – a concept which can, of course, be interpreted in a number of ways. Athol Fitzgibbons's essay is an attempt to argue that Keynes's early idealism is a form of Platonism inherited from Moore's work, and that this Platonism had an important role in the development of Keynes's early élitist views. Moreover, because it can be argued Keynes remained an élitist throughout his life, Fitzgibbons suggests that the influence of Keynes's early beliefs retained a place in Keynes's later thinking about economic life.

The range of interpretations in these papers should provide a valuable introduction to the philosophical foundations of Keynes's economics. Keynes, like Adam Smith, Karl Marx and John Stuart Mill, was actually a philosopher–economist and must be understood as such. But it is not just an exegetical, scholarly gain to understand these foundations; coming to understand them also facilitates a better understanding of the types of influences which have been responsible for some of the greatest advances in economics. Thus, in addition to providing a better understanding of the history of economic thought, these essays provide a basis for an introduction to the type of knowledge that produces successful theories.

2. Sidgwick, Moore and Keynes: a Philosophical Analysis of Keynes's 'My Early Beliefs'

Yuichi Shionoya

INTRODUCTION

In his essay 'My Early Beliefs'[1] (written in 1938 and published in 1949; hereafter referred to as MEB) Keynes described the basic beliefs on man and society which he held in his youth. The essay focuses on the influence of a Cambridge philosopher, G.E. Moore, upon the beliefs of Keynes and his friends (members of the Apostles and the Bloomsbury group). However, there are troublesome problems with MEB. What is the purpose of the memoir? What is the difference, if any, between Keynes's beliefs and those of his friends? What is the difference, if any, between Keynes's early and later beliefs? Is Keynes's memoir really a true description of reality? Furthermore, these puzzling questions are sometimes intertwined with philosophical problems. What is the philosophical standpoint of the beliefs expressed in MEB? How is the moral philosophy in MEB related to Keynes's logic of induction in his *A Treatise on Probability* and his economics in *The General Theory?* These puzzles and complications about this work are inevitable because the essay was not written by Keynes in his youth, but after he had experienced an evolution in his own thinking and after his beliefs had moved further and further away from those of his friends.

The most appropriate approach to MEB, I propose, is to identify the inner logic of its thought, without encumbering the discussion with external considerations. Perhaps because the essay was addressed as a personal memoir to the members of the Bloomsbury group, MEB has previously been considered inappropriate for a rigorous philosophical dissection. The purpose of this essay is to demonstrate that MEB has a solid philosophical structure, and to attempt a reconstruction of MEB in

6

a manner appropriate to its philosophical content. This thus entails a theoretical discussion – one that can be more readily accomplished than might the investigation of historical questions concerning whether the reconstructed thought truly describes the views of Keynes's group, or when and to what extent Keynes deviated from it.

Although MEB should be read with reference to Moore's *Principia Ethica*, it is also illuminating to discuss Keynes and Moore in light of Sidgwick's ethical theory. Henry Sidgwick, also a Cambridge philospher, represents a culmination of nineteenth-century British moral philosophy, reconciling two conflicting schools of thought – that is, utilitarianism and intuitionism. Moore was Sidgwick's student and worked within his framework of moral philosophy. Keynes was faithful to the old-fashioned tradition of economics as a moral science, and his moral philosophy can be seen as shaped by the Sidgwick–Moore connection. In the course of our argument, we shall critically comment on R.B. Braithwaite's interpretation of MEB, which does not attempt a theoretical discussion of the essay, yet has had a great influence on discussions in this field.

KEYNES ON MOORE'S THREE THESES

Moore's *Principia Ethica* (1903) is concerned with three major questions in ethics:

1. How is good to be defined?
2. What is good in itself, or what has intrinsic value?
3. What ought we to do, or what conduct is a means to good results?

Since Keynes, in MEB, directly deals with Moore's theses concerning these questions, we shall first analyse MEB with reference to these theses in order to clarify the points of agreement and disagreement. We will then try to reconstruct Keynes's own system of moral philosophy.

Meta-ethical Intuitionism

Moore's answer to the first question is that good is a simple notion which cannot be analysed and defined. Those objects of thought, such as 'good' or 'yellow', which are themselves incapable of definition, can be perceived as self-evident only by intuition. Thus the truth or falsity of a statement in which good is predicate can be known ultimately only by intuition.

This standpoint is now termed intuitionism in meta-ethics. While intuitionism has a long tradition among British moralists, it was Henry Sidgwick who distinguished between intuitionism in meta-ethics and intuitionism in normative ethics, the latter being better called deontology. Although Moore became more famous for the indefinability thesis than his teacher, he was only following Sidgwick in maintaining the indefinability of good, as Moore himself acknowledged (Moore, 1903, p. 17).

It is quite important clearly to understand the two meanings of intuitionism which modern ethics has differentiated in line with Sidgwick's insight. To use his own words, he distinguished between intuitionism in the narrower and wider sense. In the narrower, or traditional, sense intuitionism is 'the view of ethics which regards as the practically ultimate end of moral actions their conformity to certain rules or dictates of Duty unconditionally prescribed (Sidgwick, 1907, p. 96). In this view, some kinds of action are directly and immediately judged morally right without consideration of their consequences. Intuitionism in this sense is deontology and is contrasted with teleology or consequentialism. On the other hand, in the wider sense proposed by Sidgwick, intuitionism does not prescribe anything in particular, but indicates the general source and ground of moral judgements: it is the view that identifies intuition with 'immediate judgment as to what ought to be done or aimed at' (Ibid., p. 97). Thus, intuitionism in this sense is contrasted with inferentialism. It might be said that intuitionism in the narrower sense concerns the character of right action, while intuitionism in the wider sense concerns the character of the activity of making a moral judgement (Raphael, 1974, p. 406). The latter is wider than the former because it can be applied to any doctrine of normative ethics, even doctrines other than deontology. It is in this wider sense that Sidgwick and Moore are called intuitionists. In normative ethics they are both utilitarians, although their conceptions of utility differ. With regard to intuitionism in the narrower sense, Sidgwick identifies it with commonsense morality, which is, in his view, ultimately reducible to utilitarianism, but Moore definitely rejects it because the question of what we ought to do can be answered on the basis of the knowledge concerning the consequences of an action.

Roy Harrod notes there were different interpretations at Oxford and Cambridge of Moore's intuitionism and, more specifically, his doctrine of indefinability (Harrod, 1951, p. 77). In Cambridge, Harrod observes, intuitionism provided complete licence to ignore conventions and to judge all things anew, and this was the view of Keynes and his Cambridge circle of friends of Moore's doctrine. In Oxford, on the other hand, the source of moral judgement was believed to lie in the moral convictions of thoughtful and well-educated people. What ought to be done was prescribed by conventional morality, which embodied the intuitions of many generations. Such divergent interpretations of intuitionism, I argue, derived from emphasis being placed either on the meta-ethical level or on the normative level. It is worth noting that the different interpretations at Cambridge and Oxford were reflective of an apparent awkwardness in Moore's coordinating meta-ethical intuitionism with normative utilitarian ethics. Moore's doctrine of indefinability was extended from the notion of good to the notion of right by intuitionists in Oxford, such as H.A. Prichard and W.D. Ross: a right action is one that is judged by its conformity to duty or rules, without any reference to the consequences of an action. Thus, at Oxford, intuitionist meta-ethics was combined with intuitionist normative ethics, with particular emphasis on the latter. As we shall see, Keynes believed that the intuitionist meta-ethics and consequentialist normative ethics in Moore's moral philosophy were incompatible. He offered an alternative unity of the two levels of intuitionism, based on meta-ethical grounds.

Whereas the impact of Moore's thesis on the indefinability of good on Keynes and his group appears quite clear and intense – this is the central theme of MEB – Braithwaite sees things differently:

> This thesis in the logic of ethics has been of great interest to academic philosophers; but it was not one to excite the young Keynes. What excited him was what he calls the 'religion', contained in the last chapter [Chapter VI of *Principia Ethica*] – the list of things good in themselves, good for their own sakes (Harrod, 1951, p. 77).

I do not believe this is correct. Indeed, Braithwaite does not mean that Keynes did not accept the indefinability thesis, but that its basic importance in organizing Keynes's early beliefs should be properly recognized. On the basis of the indefinability thesis, Keynes developed not only his view of ideals and morals, but also his theory of probability. Keynes writes:

> How did we know what states of mind were good? This was a matter of direct inspection, of direct unanalysable intuition about which it was useless and impossible to argue (MEB, p. 437).

After illustrating a variety of ways for members of his group to handle a situation when there was a difference of opinion, Keynes concludes:

Yet after all the differences were about details. Broadly speaking we all knew for certain what were good states of mind and that they consisted in communion with objects of love, beauty and truth (MEB, p 438).

Although these passages already argue that certain states of kind are good, they also show that the judgement of what is intrinsically good is given by our intuition, and that the judgement thus obtained is considered certain. Keynes emphasizes the confidence of his group in this intuitive ability. He describes intuition and goodness perceived by intuition as follows:

> We regarded all this as entirely rational and scientific in character. Like any other branch of science, it was nothing more than the application of logic and rational analysis to the material presented as sense-data. Our apprehension of good was exactly the same as our apprehension of green, and we purported to handle it with the same logical and analytical technique which was appropriate to the latter (MEB, p. 438).

This description correctly implies that meta-ethical intuitionism is a form of cognitivism, which holds that moral judgements are a kind of knowledge which prove to be true or false. We can thus conclude from the above that Keynes accepted the essence of Moore's meta-ethical intuitionism.

Non-hedonism

The second thesis in Moore's *Principia Ethica* concerns the question: 'What is good in itself?' As mentioned above, this question is answered by intuition. Moore rejects the traditional utilitarian standpoint, especially that of Sidgwick, which regards pleasure as the sole good, and in contrast holds that the most valuable things, or those which have the greatest intrinsic value, are certain states of consciousness, specifically 'the pleasures of human intercourse and the enjoyment of beautiful objects (Moore, 1903, p. 188). Moore's position in this regard is generally termed ideal utilitarianism, implying a criticism of hedonistic utilitarianism.

Chapter VI of *Principia Ethica*, entitled 'The Ideal', develops Moore's second thesis, which Keynes calls his 'religion' in contrast with his 'morals'. The following is the key passage indicating Keynes's acceptance and rejection of Moore's views:

Now what we got from Moore was by no means entirely what he offered us. He had one foot on the threshold of the new heaven, but the other foot in Sidgwick and the Benthamite calculus and the general rules of correct behaviour. There was one chapter [Chapter V] in the *Principia* of which we took not the slightest notice. We accepted Moore's religion, so to speak, and discarded his morals. Indeed, in our opinion, one of the greatest advantages of his religion, was that it made morals unnecessary – meaning by 'religion' one's attitude towards oneself and the ultimate and by 'morals' one's attitude towards the outside world and the intermediate (MEB, p. 436).

Keynes refers to love, beauty and truth as the ideal or 'religion' of his group:

> The appropriate subjects of passionate contemplation and communion were a beloved person, beauty and truth, and one's prime objects in life were love, the creation and enjoyment of aesthetic experience and the pursuit of knowledge (MEB, pp. 436–7).

He emphasizes that, in pursuit of the good, he also followed Moore in rejecting Benthamite hedonism:

> I do now regard that [the Benthamite tradition] as the worm which has been gnawing at the insides of modern civilisation and is responsible for its present moral decay. We used to regard the Christians as the enemy, because they appeared as the representatives of tradition, convention and hocus-pocus. In truth it was the Benthamite calculus, based on an over-valuation of the economic criterion, which was destroying the quality of the popular Ideal (MEB, pp. 445–6).

The Apostles were apt to use Moore's ideal as a pretext for their unrestrained life and a 'supreme self-confidence, superiority and contempt towards all the rest of the unreconverted world' (MEB, p. 442). Bertrand Russell, an earlier member of the Apostles, about the same age as Moore but older than Keynes by about 10 years, noticed the change of attitude in the younger Apostles:

> The tone of the generation some ten years junior to my own was set mainly by Lytton Strachey and Keynes. It is surprising how great a change in mental climate those ten years had brought. We were still Victorian; they were Edwardian. We believed in ordered progress by means of politics and free discussion. The more self-confident among us may have hoped to be leaders of the multitude, but none of us wished to be divorced from it. The generation of Keynes and Lytton did not seek to preserve any kinship with the Philistine. They aimed rather at a life of retirement among fine shades and nice feelings, and conceived of the good as consisting in the passionate mutual admirations

of a clique of the elite. This doctrine, quite unfairly, they fathered upon G.E. Moore, whose disciples they professed to be. Keynes, in his memoir 'Early Beliefs' has told of their admiration for Moore's doctrine. Moore gave due weight to morals and by his doctrine of organic unities avoided the view that the good consists of a series of isolated passionate moments, but those who considered themselves his disciples ignored this aspect of his teaching and degraded his ethics into advocacy of a stuffy girls-school sentimentalizing (Russell, 1967, pp. 70–1).

As seen from Russell's strong criticism, the pursuit of the 'ideal' by the new generation of the Apostles deviated from Moore's 'morals'. The deviation of Keynes's group from Moore's 'morals' was indicative of the latent philosophical incompatibility of Moore's intuitionism with conventional morality.

Before we proceed to the problem of 'morals', or Moore's third thesis, we must discuss the significance for ethical theory of his conception of intrinsic goodness as lying in mental states or states of consciousness, rather than in a flow of pleasure. The object of Moore's criticism was Sidgwick's hedonism. Among three common notions of ultimate reasons for action – that is, pleasure, excellence, and duty – Sidgwick accepted pleasure as the sole, ultimate reason, and gave it a hedonistic formulation. It will be useful to indicate his definition of excellence or perfection: 'an ideal complex of mental qualities, of which we admire and approve the manifestation in human life' (Sidgwick, 1907, p. 10). This threefold difference in the conception of the ultimate reasons for action corresponds to fundamental distinctions in the characterization of human beings - that is, desire, existence, and action (Ibid., p. 78). Sidgwick, lumping together the pair-notions 'excellence–existence' and 'duty–action', subordinated them to the pair-notion 'pleasure–desire' and gave them the status of a means to the latter within his consequentialist or teleological framework. On the other hand, Moore, in his own teleological framework, attached much more fundamental importance to the pair 'excellence–existence' than to 'pleasure–desire'. Schneewind suggests that, although Sidgwick included the possible goal of excellence in deontological duty, it was possible to regard excellence as a non-hedonistic teleological goal (Schneewind, 1977, p. 202). This is what Moore actually did. For Moore, what has intrinsic value is not a stream of happiness abstracted from the consciousness of other things but 'many complicated states of mind' occurring in the whole existence of a man as a permanent entity (Moore, 1903, pp. 95–6). The ground for this probably derives from his principle of organic unity. Despite the difference in their treatment of excellence and pleasure, both Sidgwick and Moore relegated the pair 'duty–action' to the position of a means to an end. As we shall see in connection with Moore's third theme, the notions of duty and rules play an important instrumental role in his ethical theory in the same way as in Sidgwick's, because both claimed that commonsense morality, as the precepts of duty and rules, would lead to the greatest good.

In contrast to the teleological framework of Sidgwick and Moore, however, Keynes's non-hedonism does not admit the use of the pair 'duty–action' as a means to 'excellence–existence'. As Keynes notes:

> These states of mind were not associated with action or achievement or with consequences. They consisted in timeless, passionate states of contemplation and communion, largely unattached to 'before' and 'after'. Their value depended, in accordance with the principle of organic unity, on the state of affairs as a whole which could not be usefully analysed into parts (MEB, p. 436).

Moore's principle of organic unity was derived, in the discussion of the states of mind which have intrinsic value, as a corollary of intuitionism in opposition to inferentialism. But he remained within the teleological structure and did not doubt the compatibility of cause-and-effect relations with intrinsic good.

To summarize, with regard to Moore's second thesis, Keynes accepted Moore's non-hedonism, and what Moore and Keynes regarded as having intrinsic value is comparable to Sidgwick's notion of excellence or perfection. We already have suggested that Keynes's conception of excellence caused him to deviate from the teleological framework of Sidgwick and Moore, and this is the question to which we now turn.

Consequentialism and Rulism

The third thesis in Moore's ethical inquiry concerns the question: 'What ought we to do, or what is a right action?' This is a question of 'morals' for Keynes or of 'practical ethics' for Moore, and is discussed in Chapter V, 'Ethics in Relation to Conduct', of *Principia Ethica*. Moore's answer consists of two normative propositions: first, one should act so as to produce the greatest intrinsic good; second, one should always conform to certain rules which are both generally useful and generally practised.

The first proposition is based on consequentialism, which is a general normative principle stating that the right act is that which will produce the best overall outcome. There can be as many different versions of consequentialism as there are criteria for evaluating overall outcomes. Utilitarianism, which allows for a variety of utility concepts to evaluate the consequences of an act, is its most familiar version; but Moore's consequentialism is characterized by the use of intrinsic good or the non-hedonistic concept of utility as the criterion of evaluation.

Consequentialism presupposes that ethical judgements depend on an investigation of causes and effects. However, because our causal knowledge is often defective, we cannot assure ourselves of the effects of every possible act in every particular situation. Moreover, because Moore's conception of good is so complex, it is virtually impossible to calculate the consequences of our actions. We must be content with causal generalizations whose validity is restricted by probability statements. Therefore Moore proposes, as a practical guide, his second normative proposition – that one should follow certain rules when two conditions are fulfilled. These conditions are that rules have generally produced the best possible results and that rules are generally observed. Sidgwick and Moore advocate commonsense morality on these grounds. Although conformity to rules would appear to be deontological ethics, for Moore, as well as Sidgwick, this is not the case, since rules are favoured only so far as they are likely to bring about the greatest amount of good. In view of the usage of rule-utilitarianism and act-utilitarianism in modern ethics, we may coin the term 'rulism', or rule-ethics, to represent Moore's second proposition. Moore's two normative propositions in combination lead to ideal rule-utilitarianism.

It should not be said, however, that Moore in *Principia Ethica* was a rule-utilitarian rather than an act-utilitarian, since he urged conformity to rules only when the conditions of general utility and the general observance of rules are satisfied. In fact, Moore admits that these conditions are not generally satisfied, and that difficult cases frequently arise. Proofs of general utility are difficult even for generally observed rules, as is seen by the fact that they can lead to very different types of outcomes. Moreover, with regard to those rules which are not generally observed, it is doubtful whether a case for their general utility can be conclusively made. Thus Moore concludes:

> The individual can therefore be confidently recommended *always* to conform to rules which are both generally useful and generally practised. In the case of rules of which the general observance *would* be useful but does not exist, or of rules which are generally practised but which are not useful, no such universal recommendations can be made (Moore, 1903, p. 164).

It seems, therefore, that in case of doubt, instead of following rules, of which he is unable to see the good effects in his particular case, the individual should rather guide his choice by a direct consideration of the intrinsic value or vileness of the effects which his action may produce (Ibid., p. 166).

We could say that Moore in *Principia Ethica* was partly a rule-utilitarian and partly an act-utilitarian, but this position is theoretically weak and practically unreliable. Although rules do play a part both in rule-utilitarianism and act-utilitarianism, the meaning of a rule is quite different in each (Rawls, 1955). In act-utilitarianism, rules are simply summaries of past decisions arrived at by the direct application of the utilitarian principle to particular cases. One is allowed to deviate from such rules-of-thumb if a deviation will achieve a better result than the observance of them. By contrast, in rule-utilitarianism, rules stipulate a class of actions which is justified on utilitarian grounds, and there is simply no exception to rules. Thus, faced by rules which occasionally lead to bad outcomes, one would be at a loss concerning what to do, because one cannot differentiate between binding and non-binding rules.

It is therefore important to reconsider how act- and rule-utilitarianism can be conceptually consistent in Moore's ethics. Urmson has argued that 'Moore's act-utilitarian thesis is primarily concerned with the rightness of actions and the rule-utilitarian thesis is primarily concerned with the justification of actions' (Urmson, 1970, p. 345). I shall follow a different line of interpretation. Insofar as ethics should give an account of the rightness of an act, utilitarianism, seen as a claim of *principle*, takes the form of act-utilitarianism. Ethics as a practical art of life, however, should provide for procedures and methods for action, so that utilitarianism, seen as a claim of *practice*, would use some forms of rules. So-called rule-utilitarianism and the use of rules-of-thumb are interpreted as one of these forms.

Although Moore was unaware of the distinct concepts of rules made explicit by Rawls, he in fact dealt with them unconsciously in different contexts. By arguing that whether an act is right or wrong is a problem of empirical generalization concerning the rightness of a class of acts and not a single act, he was led to an inductive conception of rules. Problems of probability as a relative frequency emerge with respect to the consequences of an action conforming or not conforming to rules. In this context, Moore is an act-utilitarian, even when he advocates the following of rules. But Moore also maintains that one should not break certain rules. The reason for claiming absolute conformity to rules is not given by the frequency conception of probability, which allows deviation from rules on act-utilitarian grounds. Because of the weakness of his theory, Moore could not argue satisfactorily the need and utility of absolute conformity to rules under certain conditions. In his later book, *Ethics* (1912), Moore completely rejected rule-utilitarianism in favour of act-utilitarianism, which he conceived of as not only a principle but also as a practice. But the shift of position from the *Principia* to the *Ethics* is not a simple transition from rule-utilitarianism to act-utilitarianism, as Bateman (1988) argues, because the claim of rule-utilitarianism in the *Principia* was inadequate and liable to collapse into act-utilitarianism.

At any rate, Moore's moral theory can be characterized as consequentialism and rulism, although still allowing for act-utilitarianism to some extent. In order to see Keynes's attitude towards it, the meaning of his passage which I have referred to as the key passage of MEB should be clarified. In that passage Keynes declared that 'we accepted Moore's religion, so to speak, and discarded his morals'. Preceding it, he wrote:

> Now what we got from Moore was by no means entirely what he offered us. He had one foot on the threshold of the new heaven, but the other foot in Sidgwick and the Benthamite calculus and the general rules of correct behaviour (p. 436).

There is thus no doubt that the former foot of Moore relates to 'religion' or ideals and the latter to 'morals'. Moore's 'morals', discarded by Keynes's group, are specified by three notions: Sidgwick, the Benthamite calculus and the general rules of correct behaviour.

As mentioned above, Moore rejected hedonism in his discussion of intrinsic good in the sphere of the ideal. For this reason he was praised for putting 'one foot on the threshold of the new heaven'. Keynes's remark that Moore relied on 'Sidgwick and the Benthamite calculus' does not mean that Moore accepted their hedonism; it refers to Moore's acceptance of their consequentialism in the sphere of morals. Although Moore rejected the hedonism shared by both Bentham and Sidgwick, he adhered to their consequentialism, and developed what has been called an ideal utilitarianism. Finally, the term 'the general rules of correct behaviour' signifies rulism, which we specified was another element of Moore's 'morals'. Thus, it follows that Keynes's remark about discarding Moore's 'morals' means discarding Moore's consequentialism and rulism; Keynes's renunciation of Benthamism entails breaking away from Benthamite hedonism and consequentialism.

Also demonstrating Keynes's rejection of Moore's 'morals', is his statement that his group 'set on one side' two parts of Chapter V of Moore's book. The first is 'that part...which dealt with the obligation so to act as to produce by causal connection the most probable maximum of eventual good through the whole procession of future ages', and the other 'the part which discussed the duty of the individual to obey general rules' (MEB, p. 446). The former is concerned with consequentialism; the latter with rulism.

BRAITHWAITE ON KEYNES

In the above discussion of Moore's first thesis, I argued that Braithwaite belittled the impact of the indefinability thesis on the young Keynes, and that he underestimated the basic importance of meta-ethical intuitionism in Keynes's moral philosophy. We shall now examine Braithwaite's interpretation of MEB concerning Moore's second and third theses. Contrary to Keynes's own clear statement and our conclusions, Braithwaite asserts that Keynes discarded hedonism, not consequentialism. Moreover, Braithwaite does not recognize another important aspect of Keynes's early beliefs – the rejection of rulism.

In a short obituary of Keynes, Braithwaite wrote that 'his [Keynes's] own ethics was essentially that of Moore's *Principia Ethica*. Never has there been a more humane Utilitarian' (Braithwaite, 1946, p. 283). This remark clearly conflicts with Keynes's own view in MEB. In fact, when MEB was posthumously published in 1949, Braithwaite was greatly surprised to find Keynes stating his escape from Moore's ethics. The crux of the issue for Braithwaite was whether Keynes was right in saying, in the above quoted passage, that 'we accepted Moore's religion, so to speak, and discarded his morals'. This statement was made in MEB as the essential position of his group. Nevertheless, Braithwaite regards Keynes's description as a 'puzzling account', and even goes on to maintain the opposite to what Keynes clearly stated.

Concerning the consequentialist chapter (Chapter V) of *Principia Ethica*, Braithwaite does not take Keynes's decisively negative statement as seriously as his more moderate ones: 'There was one chapter in the *Principia* of which we took not the slightest notice' (MEB, p. 436), or 'we did not pay attention to this aspect of the book or bother much about it' (MEB, p. 446). Braithwaite explains why Keynes did not discard consequentialism as follows:

> My explanation is that the consequentialist teaching in *Principia Ethica* was
> not exhilarating novelty, since it was part of the classical Utilitarianism which
> Keynes had absorbed throughout his childhood. Moore's influence made him
> spew out the hedonism, but left the consequentialism intact. (Braithwaite,
> 1975, p. 244)

If this reasoning were correct, it would follow that Keynes, brought up
in classical economics, would not have criticized it at all. Further,
Braithwaite's interpretation would not adequately explain Keynes's
denial of another strand of classical utilitarianism – that is, hedonism –
although Moore's influence was alluded to as its cause. Indeed,
Braithwaite was compelled to attribute Keynes's critique of classical
utilitarianism to a 'personal factor', that Sidgwick's personality was
unattractive.

Keynes in MEB explicitly rejects Benthamism and the Benthamite
calculus. Benthamism or classical utilitarianism is conceptually composed
of consequentialism and hedonism. On the above ground, Braithwaite
insists that Keynes's rejection of Benthamism did not cover its
consequentialist aspect. Yet Braithwaite's argument that Keynes never
departed from consequentialist moral philosophy is far from convinc-
ing. Keynes emphasizes that his group neglected and discarded
consequentialist morality. More important is the internal consistency of
Keynes's philosophical views on meta-ethics, 'religion' and 'morals'.
On the relationship between 'religion' and 'morals' Keynes says: 'one
of the greatest advantages of his [Moore's] religion was that it made
morals unnecessary' (MEB, p. 436). And on the relationship between
meta-ethics and 'morals': 'We entirely repudiated a personal liability on
us to obey general rules. We claimed the right to judge every individual
case on its merits, and the wisdom, experience and self-control to do so
successfully' (MEB, p. 446). Insofar as one can judge goodness or
badness, rightness or wrongness by intuition in the meta-ethical sense,
one does not need any conventional rules of morality.

Braithwaite scarcely recognizes the weight of Keynes's non-rulism
and its relation to intuitionism. He de-emphasizes Keynes's repudiation
of rulism by interpreting it to mean that every general rule must have
exceptions; he also de-emphasizes Keynes's declaration of intuitionism
by interpreting it as a claim to liberty of conscience. But Keynes's claim
for intuitive judgements of particular cases depends on a belief in
intuitive ability and leads necessarily to the denial of general rules.
Fitzgibbons correctly criticizes Braithwaite for giving a psychological,
rather than an analytical, discussion of why Keynes misrepresented his

own philosophy (Fitzgibbons, 1988, p. 94). It is important for us to try to understand what Keynes actually said so as to reconstruct his coherent system of moral philosophy.

KEYNES'S INTUITIONISM

To take a step forward, we shall consider the structure of Keynes's moral theory and specifically how his non-consequentialism and non-rulism can be incorporated into an ethical theory. In the above we have referred to Sidgwick's ethics as a conceptual framework by which one can interpret some aspects of Moore and Keynes. We shall now resume this thread of the argument to develop an integrated picture of Keynes's moral theory.

The foregoing discussions are summarized in following Table 2.1 in which we compare Sidgwick, Moore, and Keynes with regard to three basic issues in ethics – namely, meta-ethics (how a moral judgement is justified), the ideal or value (what is good) and the morality of action (what should be done). The separation of moral principle from moral practice is also useful.

It is a distinct feature of Sidgwick's synthesis of intuitionism and utilitarianism that hedonistic utilitarianism is supported by both meta-ethics and practical ethics: on the one hand, utilitarianism is justified by intuitively self-evident axioms, and on the other, it is furnished with conventional commonsense morality as a practical guide. In other words, Sidgwick's hedonistic utilitarianism is supported by a meta-ethical intuitionism and a practical rulism (or ethical intuitionism).

Table 2.1   Comparison of Sidgwick, Moore and Keynes in three basic issues of ethics

	Sidgwick	Moore	Keynes
Meta-ethics:	Intuitionism	= Intuitionism	= Intuitionism
The ideal:	Pleasure	↔Excellence	= Excellence
The morality of action:			
Principle:	Consequentialism =Consequentialism	↔ Nonconsequentialism
Practice:	Rulism	= Rulism	↔ Non-rulism
(= indicates sameness of positions; ↔ difference of positions)			

Moore inherited this structure from Sidgwick except for the rejection of hedonism, although, unlike Sidgwick, he did not identify his rulism with ethical intuitionism. This is a modification within the consequentialist framework: pleasure as the ultimate end was replaced with excellence (that is, truth, love, and beauty). In MEB, Keynes repudiated Moore's consequentialism and rulism, thereby destroying the consequentialist moral framework and its conventional moral guide. For Keynes, it was meta-ethical intuition that filled this vacuum in the sphere of morality; and he asserted that intuition determined not only what is good, but also what should be done in principle and in practice. Keynes's ethical model was the result of a thorough, logical application of meta-ethical intuitionism not only to the conception of ideal but also to moral principle and practice. Moore's return to full act-utilitarianism from partial rule-utilitarianism in his *Ethics* might well reflect the impact of Keynes's critique; strangely enough, however, while he retained act-consequentialism in his Ethics, he did not solve the problem of the incalculability of the consequences of action, which was the real ground of rulism in *Principia Ethica*.

With regard to Keynes's non-consequentialism, we shall discuss some further points. First, Keynes developed a critique of the consequentialist aspect of utilitarianism on four points in *Probability* (Keynes, 1921, VIII, pp. 343–9). He took issue with the assumptions, first, that goodness is numerically measurable and arithmetically additive and, second, that probability is also numerically measurable. Under these assumptions mathematical expectation of alternative actions provides measures for the choice of actions. Even if the first assumption is justified, he argues, the second is not, because a probability is a degree of belief based on certain premises so that the outcomes of a different series of premises are not comparable. Third, even if we were to know mathematical expectation, consideration of alternative actions on that ground does not involve the weights of the arguments – namely, the amount of evidence upon which each probability is based. Fourth, they also ignore the elements of risk – namely, the undesirability attendant on the uncertain worst case.

Of all these points, the second is the most important from an epistemological point of view, since it raises the question of whether the concept of probability should be formulated as the frequency of occurrence, as in utilitarianism, or as the degree of belief one holds in a hypothesis given some evidence, as in Keynes's *Treatise on Probability*. Keynes's conception of probability introduces intuitive judgements into uncertain situations in place of consequentialist calculation: indeed, it can be said that it is the foundation of Keynes's non-consequentialism.

Second, the idea of consequentialism is so attractive because it says that one ought to do what minimizes evil and maximizes good, or what produces the best overall outcome. But non-consequentialism does not imply any deliberate irrationality in decision-making, since it is quite natural to take consequences into consideration when they are evident. Keynes says: 'The consequences of being found out had, of course, to be considered for what they were worth' (MEB, p. 446). What matters is how to approach the uncertain world. He denied the consequentialist approach that estimates the consequences by mathematical expectation. When consequences are certain – that is, when premises entail their consequences – it would be trivial to take them into consideration.

Third, non-consequentialism may mislead some people. So long as we try to achieve desirable outcomes, it seems natural for us to act with prospective consequences in mind. But this is not what Keynes means by consequentialism. Indeed, although both Moore and Keynes regard certain 'states of kind' as having intrinsic goodness, this does not necessarily mean that they adopt a consequentialist morality. The problem is how to judge the outcomes. As we noted above, consequentialism is a doctrine of inferentialism to the extent that it judges the relations between actions and consequences by inference. Keynes, in contrast, tries to grasp the ideal 'states of kind' not by inference but by intuition. MEB states that Keynes and his friends discussed the 'problems of mensuration' (p. 440); but this is actually concerned with the intuitive evaluation of outcomes as such, not with the inferential evaluation of the relations between causes and effects or between means and ends. Thus, it might be said, that the problem is a matter of definition of the word consequentialism. If so, consequentialism based on inferentialism should somehow be distinguished from consequentialism based on intuitionism. I call the latter non-consequentialism.

Fourth, Keynes interprets the overall understanding of the states of mind in terms of the principle of organic unity through time. This should be interpreted to avoid judgements based on the impulse of the moment; to use a term of British moral philosophy, it is a principle of prudence. Sidgwick elevated this idea of prudence into a self-evident axiom in meta-ethics. Thus the principle of organic unity shared by Moore and Keynes regards an impartial interest in one's own good at different times as intuitively rational.

Let us turn to another distinct element in Keynes's moral theory – non-rulism. His attitude towards the rulism of Sidgwick and Moore took the form of denial. 'We repudiated entirely customary morals, conventions and traditional wisdom. We were, that is to say, in the strict sense of the term, immoralists' (MEB, p. 446). Why did Keynes and his group reject rules in judging what to do? How did they behave when they rejected rules? The answer lies in their confidence in intuition. Confidence in intuitive ability coupled with the conception of the intrinsic good as complex 'states of mind' leads to non-rulism. In other words, Keynes's non-rulism is based on meta-ethical intuitionism as the source of moral judgements and on the concept of excellence intuitively grasped as the ultimate good. As we have seen, confidence in intuition explains the self-evidence of the ultimate good. Further, the concept of excellence in states of mind as a whole exorcises both consequentialism and rulism. Sidgwick and Moore kept consequentialism and rulism compatible with intuitionism; in Keynes, however, intuitionism precludes these two moral positions. Intuition enables one to make fresh moral judgements without relying on conventions. This is what Keynes's term 'immoralists' means; it does not mean that Keynes and his group did not have any morality.

Keynes's position in ethics can be expressed as 'perceptional intuitionism', to use Sidgwick's classic terminology once again. Sidgwick (1907, p. 102) distinguished three phases or species of intuitionism in the meta-ethical sense – perceptional, dogmatic, and philosophical – which indicate three stages in the formal development of intuitive morality. What is common to all three is that the rightness of a moral statement is judged intuitively – that is, immediately without further inference. The difference among the phases is due to the difference of generality in the moral statements intuitively given.

According to perceptional intuitionism, the rightness of particular actions is held to be immediately known. Particular judgements may differ according to particular cases and particular persons. Dogmatic intuitionism establishes general rules or conventions by which certain classes of acts are intuitively judged to be right, this being the standard method of ethical intuitionism which is identified with the morality of common sense or duty. Philosophical intuitionism brings out a few self-evident axioms which are acceptable to the most fundamental intuition. Whereas the dictates in the first and second forms of intuitionism make it possible to evaluate particular acts, philosophical intuitionism gives axioms from which some ethical systems might be deduced and on which they might be grounded. Keynes had confidence in the intuitive ability of judgements in particular cases of individual action without relying on rules. Keynes may therefore be called a perceptional, rather than dogmatic, intuitionist.

By 1938 Keynes had come to accept some criticism of his early beliefs which had been earlier suggested by D.H. Lawrence. MEB was in fact motivated by Keynes's self-criticism of his non-rulism and, in particular, of his perceptional intuitionism. His concluding remark runs:

> We were not aware that civilisation was a thin and precarious crust erected by the personality and the will of a very few, and only maintained by rules and conventions skilfully put across and guilefully preserved. We had no respect for traditional wisdom or the restraints of custom... [W]e completely misunderstood human nature, including our own. The rationality which we attributed to it led to a superficiality, not only of judgment, but also of feeling (MEB, pp. 447–8).

Here, rationality refers to the intuitive ability of judgements or, more precisely, to perceptional intuitionism.

The underlying purpose in Sidgwick's intuitionism is to define right and good by reason or rationality in each phase of intuitionism. In Sidgwick, the concept of rightness applies not only to the fitness of means to given ends, but also to certain kinds of actions without regard to consequences and to the adoption of certain ends themselves. Of these three usages, the first is the classical conception of rationality, defined as a choice of the optimum means to given ends, while the second is concerned with duty, commonly held to be right in itself. But because, for Sidgwick, duty is to be defined as a means to the good, rationality in the second usage is reduced to the first. The third usage relates to the rightness of ultimate ends. Evaluation of ends by rationality means rationality is logically prior to the good.

The most crucial philosophical problem in Sidgwick's intuitionism was to explain the rightness of ultimate ends in terms of rationality. Since rightness is concerned with the optimum means to given ends, it is reductively explained by the goodness of ends. But where rightness applies to ends as such, it is ultimate and unanalysable. It is here that Moore became famous for the doctrine of the indefinability of good. Unlike Moore, Sidgwick tried to explain the rightness of ends in light of rationality, and put forward, as self-evident axioms, what might be called a structure of rationality in the phase of philosophical intuitionism.

In Sidgwick's system of ethics there are thus three kinds of intuitive rationality according to the three phases of intuitionism. We argue that the central problems in Keynes's early beliefs and his later self-criticism are concerned with the relative importance to be given to the different kinds of rationality corresponding to the phases of perceptional and dogmatic intuitionism. Indeed, we might add that Keynes's work on probability, inspired by Moore's proposition about 'probable' and 'ought', was an attempt at an axiomatic formulation of philosophical intuitionism. Keynes's intuitionist ethics might thus seem to fall broadly within the intuitionist framework plotted by Sidgwick: between immediate judgements and conventional rules. Although intuition and rules might appear to conflict with each other, they are both basically regulated by rationality. Keynes's work on probability can be understood as an inquiry into the structure of rationality involved in immediate judgements, while his work in economics was an attempt at proposals for rational rules of a society. In this sense, the intuitionist framework of Sidgwick and Moore which Keynes encountered in his early days was the source of much of his subsequent intellectual activity in probability and economics. However, in order to develop our argument, we must introduce politics and discuss the relation between ethics and politics.

ETHICS AND POLITICS

An important problem remains in MEB which should be clarified: the relationship between ethics and politics. The relevance of this problem to our discussion can be stated as follows. First, Braithwaite's interpretation that Keynes was a consequentialist rests on the former's failure to distinguish between ethics and politics and between individual action and public policy. From Keynes's contribution to public policy, based on the science of expediency, Braithwaite simply concluded that Keynes misrepresented his own standpoint, whereas Keynes, in MEB, was in fact concerned with individual non-consequentialist morality.

Second, a recent study of Keynes's early writings concludes that Keynes learned from Edmund Burke that the science of politics was a doctrine of expediency, a doctrine of means (Skidelsky, 1983, pp. 154–60). Thus, the relation between Burke's politics and Moore's ethics adds a new dimension to the understanding of Keynes's early beliefs. This problem is directly related to the question of whether Keynes was a consequentialist, and whether he could be said to be a political utilitarian.

I suspect, however, that this new dimension, lacking a clear recognition of the relation between ethics and politics, confuses rather than clarifies the matter.

Third, while I have used Sidgwick's ethical theory as a framework for discussing the ethics of Moore and Keynes, it is also of value in analysing Keynes's own view of politics. Sidgwick clearly distinguished between ethics and politics, both of which are concerned with 'ought': 'Ethics aims at determining what ought to be done by individuals, while Politics aims at determining what the government of a state or political society ought to do and how it ought to be constituted' (Sidgwick, 1907, p.15). This definition is not necessarily followed today, because ethics is often thought to concern the principles that govern the basic structure of a society, so that there is little difference between contemporary moral philosophy and political philosophy. But Keynes sticks strictly to Sidgwick's distinction. Thus, unless they are aware of this distinction, modern commentators on Keynes are liable to be misled.

Fourth, the concept of politics is essential to an understanding of rules, because rules presuppose a society. Thus, the question of how individuals ought to behave in relation to rules and customs (this question relates to one of Sidgwick's ultimate reasons for action – that is, duty) is closely related to the question of how a society ought to be constituted. The link between ethics and politics is provided by the existence of a society, which is more or less deliberately designed, and in wh:ch certain moral values are established and become a duty for individuals in that society.

Our preceding conclusion that Keynes's meta-ethical intuitionism brought about his non-consequentialism and non-rulism is maintained as a proposition in the realm of ethics. Opponents of this conclusion would claim non-consequentialism and non-utilitarianism are absurd, because they confuse ethics and politics, although their confusion might be sustained and concealed by common sense. In fact, the world of ethics depicted in MEB was so unworldly that it would be difficult to correctly understand Keynes's statements. Keynes emphasizes the unworldliness of Moore's ethical ideal which he and his circle enthusiastically accepted, although he mentions that he himself was conscious of the secular world:

[O]ur religion was altogether unworldly – with wealth, power, popularity or success it had no concern whatever, they were thoroughly despised (MEB, p. 437).

The New Testament is a handbook for politicians compared with the unworldliness of Moore's chapter on 'The Ideal' (MEB, p. 444).

We existed in the world of Plato's *Dialogues*; we had not reached the *Republic*, let alone the *Laws* (MEB, p. 445).

[S]ocial action as an end in itself and not merely as a lugubrious duty had dropped out of our Ideal, and not only social action, but the life of action generally, power, politics, success, wealth, ambition, with the economic motive and the economic criterion less prominent in our philosophy than with St Francis of Assisi, who at least made collections for the birds... (MEB, p. 445).

Non-consequentialism and non-rulism were thus the result of a thorough application of meta-ethical intuitionism to such an unworldly universe.

In this light, the relationship between ethics and politics in Sidgwick, Moore, and Keynes becomes much clearer. This can best be seen by considering the three ultimate reasons – pleasure, duty, and excellence – for action, which I referred to as one of Sidgwick's conceptual devices. As Table 2.2 indicates, Sidgwick includes excellence (in particular, moral excellence) under duty, and regards them both as a means to pleasure.

Table 2.2   Comparison of Sidgwick, Moore, and Keynes on the three ultimate reasons for action

	Sidgwick	Moore	Keynes
Ethics:			
Ends:	Pleasure	Excellence (incl. Pleasure)	Excellence (incl. Pleasure)
Means:	Duty (incl. Excellence)	Duty	–
Politics:	–	–	Duty

Duty is crystallized in commonsense morality or rules. Since Sidgwick's ethics does not presuppose an ideal form of society in the sphere of politics, duty works as an indispensable means to attain ultimate ends in the sphere of ethics. At the same time, Sidgwick regarded rules as a means to utilitarian goodness, arguing that commonsense morality is unconsciously utilitarian.

Moore kept the consequentialist framework, although he replaced pleasure with excellence; pleasure can be included in excellence as an integral part of a desirable consciousness. Being uninterested in politics, he made the distinction between ethics and politics completely obscure, discussing ethics by mixing the two issues up. Yet, if we examine Chapter V of *Principia Ethica* closely, we find that his teleological or consequentialist framework includes two steps: first, the relation between ultimate ends and all-purpose means and, second, the relation between all-purpose means and a means to them, which Moore regards as rules. The second step suggests a consequentialist formulation of politics, leading Moore to write the following remarkable passage:

> [T]hese rules, since they can be recommended as a means to that which is itself only a necessary condition for the existence of any great good, can be defended independently of correct views upon the primary ethical question of what is good in itself. On any view commonly taken, it seems certain that the preservation of civilised society, which these rules are necessary to effect, is necessary for the existence, in any great degree, of anything which may be held to be good in itself (Moore, 1903, p. 158).

The all-purpose means or, to quote from the above passage, 'that which is itself only a necessary condition for the existence of any great good' includes, according to Moore, 'the tendency to preserve and propagate life and the desire of property' (Ibid., p. 157). It should be noted that Moore's objective of rules is not utility, if his consequentialist inference is analysed in two steps.

Keynes's notion of excellence, which also includes pleasure, precludes a consequentialist consideration. There is no ends-and-means relationship in his intuitionism so far as the sphere of ethics is concerned. In Keynes, duty is relegated to the sphere of politics. Further, as an economist, he assigned rightness or rationality to rules according to non-utilitarian considerations.

If we combine ethics and politics into one in Table 2.2, Moore and Keynes might appear the same, and their differences on ethical and political principles would be certainly hidden. While Moore maintains consequentialism in ethics and politics, Keynes holds intuitionism in ethics and consequentialism in politics. The problem for Keynes is how intuitionism and consequentialism are compatible with each other. Indeed, it is because of the need to establish this compatibility that Keynes was compelled to confess in MEB the conceit of neglecting conventions and rules in the sphere of ethics. While in ethics Keynes was a full-fledged intuitionist, in the analysis of political systems he used a consequentialist approach in which the end was not a summation of individual utilities, but was defined in terms of economic and social objectives, such as full employment, price stability, and social justice. In this case, it is not appropriate to call Keynes a 'political utilitarian'. Even if Keynes and Burke emphasize instrumental expediency for promoting general happiness, this does not entail utilitarianism. The end in politics, for which expediency is required, is not directly conceived of in terms of utility but in terms of the all-purpose means to be found in the political structure. It is the problems of justice, liberty, rights and so on, not aggregate utility, that determine the political structure. Keynes's political task was the provision of what Rawls terms 'social primary goods' (Rawls, 1971). Keynes gives the most general statement on political principles as follows: 'The political problem of mankind is to combine three things: economic efficiency, social justice, and individual liberty' (Keynes, 1926, p. 311). The way these three major criteria are combined, far from being neutral as Moore innocently supposed, is subject to political ideology. By his power of insight and persuasion, Keynes struggled for a programme of rational public policy. The objective of this public policy, he firmly believed, could be conceived by intuitive rationality.

CONCLUSION

I have proposed to reconstruct the structure of Keynes's moral philosophy expressed in MEB in light of Sidgwick's ethics, whose concepts and framework are especially relevant to the thoughts of Moore and Keynes. Specifically, I have proposed to distinguish between meta-ethical intuitionism and ethical intuitionism, between inferential consequentialism and intuitive consequentialism, and between ethics and politics, and to consider intrinsic value with reference to either pleasure, or excellence, or duty. I have interpreted Keynes's ethics as an ethics of excellence, which is based on neither consequentialism nor rulism, but is totally justified by meta-ethical intuitionism. If Sidgwick represented a reconciliation of two dominant schools of thought in moral philosophy – ethical intuitionism and utilitarianism – by means of meta-ethical intuitionism, Keynes attempted a renunciation of both ethical intuitionism and utilitarianism by means of meta-ethical intuitionism.

In ethics, Keynes was not a utilitarian because he refuted consequentialism and hedonism; his ethics was that of excellence or perfection combined with meta-ethical intuitionism. He could thus dispense with rules in ethics. Keynes's political philosophy, however, was definitely concerned with the provision of rules. In order to assess the nature of rules it was necessary to see the ends behind the rules in question. Neither was Keynes a utilitarian in politics. His political philosophy does not define a social goal in terms of utility, and goes no further than a provision of instrumental or 'social primary' goods to a good life. On the basis of an efficient, just and liberal framework of a society, ethical intuitions are left to determine the ultimate ends of individuals. This is the hierarchical relation between ethics and politics in Keynes.

NOTE

1. Page references to 'My Early Beliefs' in the *Collected Writings*, vol. X are given in the text.

3.   Burke and Keynes[1]

Suzanne Helburn

In his biography of Keynes, Robert Skidelsky alludes to the importance of Edmund Burke in the formation of Keynes's political philosophy. He notes that:

> Keynes never wrote a treatise on politics, but in his papers there is a 99 page undergraduate essay on 'The Political Doctrines of Edmund Burke'. This is his most extended treatment of the 'theory and methods of politics'. ... [Keynes thought of Burke as] one of the great political thinkers of all time. If Moore was his ethical hero, Burke may lay strong claim to be his political hero. Certainly he was the only one he ever acknowledged as such (Skidelsky, 1983, p. 154).

How is it possible that Edmund Burke, the prophet of twentieth-century conservatism, also profoundly influenced this century's quintessentially liberal economist? If Burke did indeed influence Keynes, can we trace the interplay of conservative and liberal elements in the thought of both Burke and Keynes? This paper, which is based on an analysis of Keynes's early essay on Burke, his unpublished Apostles papers, and some of his relevant later writing on politics, seeks to identify Burke's influence on Keynes's ethics and political thought.[2]

It is clear that Burke was a major influence on Keynes, and in his later essays on politics he frequently alluded to him. Often one can hear echoes of Burke both in Keynes's arguments and in his choice of concepts and issues. One word in particular, which was a favourite of Keynes, 'prejudice', he often used in the non-pejorative Burkean sense to mean natural predispositions based on habit or intuition. In fact, a possible key to Keynes's enthusiasm for Burke, despite his fundamental disagreements with him, lies in the prejudices they shared – a loathing of the bourgeois calculating spirit, a profound contempt for abstract theorizing, a love of country and of civilized sensibilities. In contrast to G. E. Moore, who is often considered the major influence on Keynes's philosophy, Burke's fundamental commitment to good government and his emphasis on the performance of one's public duty must have appealed to the young Keynes. Certainly his worldliness suited Keynes's temperament better than Moore's absorption in an intensely private world.

However, it should not be inferred from the above that Keynes indiscriminately accepted ideas from thinkers he admired, including Burke. Indeed, Keynes's early papers illustrate his independence of mind. Skidelsky alludes to Keynes's penchant for 'ruthless truthtelling' (Skidelsky, 1983, p. xxii), a method which seeks the truth by subjecting the work of other theorists to the closest scrutiny. While his attitude was respectful and open, he was nevertheless ruthless in his search for the essence and logic of their arguments, and, in particular, for tacit assumptions. He looked for flaws, not only in logic but in the intuitive reasonableness of assumptions and implications. Many of his own ideas developed through this process of subjecting the thought of others to searching intuitive introspection and analysis.

The purpose of this paper is to provide a clearer and more complete picture of Burke's influence on Keynes than has heretofore been attempted. I will show how Burke's writing influenced both Keynes's reformist and élitist politics, thus providing a basis for both liberal and conservative aspects of those politics. I will also argue that this influence goes beyond those views they shared and which Keynes directly attributes to Burke. There are many parallels between Keynes's and Burke's views on politics – for instance their views on revolution, on international relations and on the importance of faction in politics. Yet, despite these similarities, Keynes ordinarily did not accept the conservative content of Burke's politics. Rather, the most important connections derive from Keynes's acceptance of the logic of Burke's political theory – an ethically based doctrine of expediency and an élitist view about the exercise of political power. Basically, Keynes advocated a twentieth-century technocratic version of Burke's civic humanist, oligarchic rule. Thus it is plausible to argue that Keynes developed his interventionist political strategy and tactics from insights about the political process learned from Burke.

The first section gives a brief portrait of Burke's thought and summarizes the evolution of its interpretations, indicating changes in the characterizations of his political theory. It is useful to situate Keynes's Burke essay in the historical development of work on Burke because it represents a transition from nineteenth-century utilitarian to twentieth-century natural law interpretations of Burke's ethics and politics. The second section presents and analyses Keynes's principal arguments about Burke from his 1904 paper 'The Political Doctrine of Edmund Burke', his Apostles papers and his later writings on politics and ethics. It provides an analysis of the logic of Burke's political philosophy as well as Keynes's reactions to it, demonstrating Keynes's basic understanding and acceptance of the logic. It also shows how Burke's influence can be seen in Keynes's most explicitly political work, *The Economic Consequences of the Peace* and in his 1920s essays on party politics in Britain. Finally, this section identifies the bases for Keynes's major criticisms of Burke's conservative politics. The third section draws conclusions and implications.

CONFLICTING INTERPRETATIONS OF BURKE'S POLITICAL PHILOSOPHY

It is important to put Burke's writings in the context of the great debates of which they were a part – the nature and morality of the American and French revolutions, the ethical and practical issues involved in ruling a subjugated colonial people such as in India and Ireland, the importance of the English Constitution in creating a balance of power between the Crown and Parliament, the nature and possibility of good government. These debates concerned the rights, obligations and relative power of the king and his court, of the ascendant bourgeoisie, of the hereditary landed aristocracy, and the right to self-government of the people as a whole.

The philosophy of governance enunciated by Burke for the Whigs, to defend the maintenance of their power, was that of *good* government for the people as a whole – honest government to promote peace, tranquillity and the happiness of the people. To this extent, Burke was a reformer. But Burke was primarily a conservative. He worked for good government *for* the people, but not *by* the people. As Morley commented, 'everything should be done for the multitude but nothing by them' (Morley, 1879, p. 174). He saw society as a complex organic unity, organized hierarchically into different ranks, each important to the orderly functioning of the whole. Since he considered the hierarchical organization a reflection of natural order, it was thus the duty of the propertied classes to govern for the good of the whole, and the duty of the lower ranks to accept their position in the social hierarchy. Governance is effected through the constitutions of particular states which represent the embodiment and application of natural law.

People, according to Burke, are basically social beings; they find their own good tied up with that of others; they are part of and dependent on the whole; and hence they have moral obligations to their society. Since Burke accepted the existence of evil as inevitable, he considered morality as the social glue, emphasizing the importance of duties which, like human nature, he considered to be basically unchanging. Despite the relatively static implications of this view, he accepted the fact of slow, organic social change, and recognized the importance of social institutions in improving the human condition. Michael Freeman comments that, for Burke, history is the unfolding of God's will which develops the potential for goodness inherent in people; thus, it is Christianity that is the chief source of progress. Because fundamental truths develop gradually into social institutions, an ordered society is the main instrument of God's will, and order in society is evidence of the working of natural law (Freeman, 1980, p. 78).

Burke was deeply suspicious of eighteenth-century rationalism because of his view of the world as a complex, imperfect reality on which it was impossible to impose abstract ideals. The problem confronting the statesman is one of prudence or political expediency: to encourage natural social development by choosing judiciously among imperfect alternatives which necessarily represent a combination of good and evil. Any reforms should be designed so as to conserve the best traditions, social experimentation should be minimized, and revolution, which destroys the social order, is anathema. Burke opposed the democratization of politics because he considered good government hard to accomplish, and the masses of the people incompetent to pick appropriate representatives or understand complicated policy issues. He especially condemned abstract principles which posited the people's 'right' to self-rule – to him, this constituted a violation of natural law. Burleigh Wilkins says that, because Burke stipulated man's dependence on God and society, he did not recognize individual rights or duties which ignore or minimize the importance of this dependent status (Wilkins, 1967, p. 249).

Since Burke never systematized his writings on politics, scholars have had to construct his political theory from a prolific stream of parliamentary speeches, pamphlets and letters. Burke was always controversial. He was a man who held passionately to his beliefs, a man of great moral courage who considered it his duty to speak convincingly on great issues of the day. Hence, his writings are highly partisan and intentionally polemic. In addition, both his contemporaries and later interpreters accused him of inconsistency – of arbitrarily changing his positions. Finally, Burke had to respond to the political cross-currents of the time. Although he revered the traditional social order, he also valued the economic progress created by the expansion of trade. All of this has given rise to variant and conflicting interpretations.

Isaac Kramnick describes the evolving legend of Burke: in the late eighteenth century he was the heroic Tory of Wordsworth's *Prelude*; in the nineteenth century he was the Victorian liberal utilitarian; in the twentieth century he has become the prophet of conservatism, particularly in the USA (Kramnick, 1977, pp. 39–51). Kramnick points out that Burke's views have repeatedly been used to defend the political beliefs of his interpreters and to defend a capitalist world profoundly different from his own eighteenth-century society. He contends that the ambiguities in Burke's writing which make these varied interpretations possible reflect his position as a transitional figure in late eighteenth-century politics.

J.G.A. Pocock provides useful insights into the ambiguities in the eighteenth-century political discourse in which Burke participated (Pocock, 1985). He characterizes these debates as expressive of the continuing tension between 'virtue and commerce', between polity and economy, and between the discourse of ancient civic humanism or republicanism and that of jurisprudentialism. He claims that, throughout the early modern period and alongside the history of liberalism and the development of possessive individualism, there existed a history of republican civic humanism which emphasized the ancient tradition of citizenship among equals who both govern and are governed. Central to this tradition is the view that the practice of self-rule among this élite, characterized by political virtue and a devotion to the public good, is integral to the state of 'humanness'.

Pocock argues that republican virtue resurfaced in England to deal with the central question of Whig politics in the period from 1688 to 1776 and after: 'whether a regime founded on patronage, public debt, and professionalization of the armed forces did not corrupt both governors and governed'. He argues that the appearance of a new ruling élite of 'stockholders and officeholders whose relations with government were those of mutual dependence, was countered by a renewed... assertion of the ideal of the citizen', as autonomous and incorruptable because his real property (land) assured his virtue (Ibid., p. 48).

Burke's political thought developed in this milieu and certainly contains elements of civic humanism. However, he also contributed to the reconciliation of the ideals of virtue and commerce into what Pocock calls 'commercial humanism'. In this view, commerce was the force which 'refined manners and extended the sympathies' (Ibid., p. 191).

However, commercial development had implications for government as well as morality. Because the commercial class devoted its energies to business, governance became the province of a newly emerging class of civil servants. Thus, in this period, we see the early development of the technocratic élites so important to Keynes's thinking.

Despite Burke's respect for the civilizing possibilities of commerce, Pocock points out that, in the *Reflections*, he identified the dark side, recognizing the potential of commerce to destroy, rather than promote, culture and refinement. He interpreted the French Revolution as a con-spiracy of intellectuals and monied interests to take over Church lands, and he defended the older, medieval institutions as the creators and defenders of manners and culture. Although Burke might not have been the leader of the revolt against the enlightenment, Pocock says he foreshadowed the advent of the nineteenth-century conservative politics of romanticism and alienated sensibility which considered capitalist social relations 'philistine and utilitarian' (Pocock, 1985, p. 191). Again, we see a possible parallel with Keynes who also questioned the ability of capitalism to refine manners and extend the sympathies.

Several parallels exist between Burke and Keynes. First is their importance as intellectual and political leaders responding to revolution-ary change. Second, there are striking similarities in their world-view and, consequently, in their politics. These include: their view of society as a complex organic unity and, therefore, the dangers involved in applying abstract theories of amelioration in politics; their acceptance of a natural hierarchical social order and of the duty of leaders both to embody the human virtues and to control politics; their concern for good government which responds to the people's desires but limits their political power; their acceptance of individuals as social beings with its attendant necessity of limiting personal liberty.

KEYNES AND BURKE: THE 1904 ESSAY AND BEYOND

Keynes's analysis of Burke in his 1904 essay seems motivated in part by his objections to the essentially utilitarian interpretation of nineteenth-century Burke scholars such as Morley, Buckle and Lecky (Morley, 1867 and 1879; Buckle, 1904; Lecky, 1891). Although his essay preceded the twentieth-century natural law interpretations, he seems to have anticipated some of their arguments.[3]

Keynes's relationship to Burke's writings has been discussed in two recent books by Athol Fitzgibbons (Fitzgibbons, 1988) and R. M. O'Donnell (O'Donnell, 1989a). In his discussion of the influence of Burke on Keynes, Fitzgibbons accepts the recent natural law interpretation of Burke's political philosophy and argues that Keynes adopted the 'logic' of Burke's political theory – a logic based on an ethical theory of the state more akin to Platonic and Aristotelian idealist political theory than to nineteenth-century utilitarian thought (Fitzgibbons, 1988, p. 56). The analysis presented here corroborates Fitzgibbons's interpretation as well as R. M. O'Donnell's characterization of Keynes's politics as a form of political rationalism.[4]

This section contains a schematization of that logic and demonstrates that, in the 1904 essay, Keynes both recognized this logic and, for the most part, agreed with it. Furthermore, it will be shown that it forms the basis for both Keynes's liberal reform politics and his conservative élitism. However, Keynes rejected many of the maxims with which Burke is most closely associated, and, in the 1904 essay, he exposes the excesses which contributed to Burke's conservatism. This section identifies those aspects of the content of Burke's conservative politics which Keynes rejected and his reasons for considering them inadequate in the modern world.

Keynes's Acceptance of the Logic of Burke's Political Philosophy

When Burke's political philosophy is seen as based on ethics derived from natural law, the following components form a logically coherent political philosophy:

1. There are universal ethical goods, the pursuit of which defines moral duties and the embodiment of which constitutes virtue. These values and duties are based on natural law, 'the sphere of Eternal

Law accessible to man as a rational creature' (Parkin, 1956, p. 6), reflecting the existence of natural, universal characteristics of man (Wilkins, 1967, p. 248).

2. Government is not part of the good; rather it is a practical institution to 'facilitate the attainment of various private goods by the individual members of a community'. Therefore, since there is no ideal form of government, such as democracy, the 'people' have no natural right to self-government. Rather, good government is that government which fulfils its obligations to the people, and politics is a science of means (Keynes, 1904c, p. 6).

3. Practical politics should be based on the principle of expediency – that is, the practice of steering a course between the immediate desires of the people and what is ethical and, hence, rational.

4. Political authority must be vested in a natural élite capable of promoting popular desires while preserving and promoting the good. Democratic institutions check the power of political authority and make the latter ultimately accountable to the people. Although the extent of democracy must be limited, it cannot be determined abstractly; it must be a matter of compromise.

5. Excellence in political leadership involves the classic virtues of moral courage, moderation, wisdom, and commitment to a life of action for the general good, as well as a disregard of personal reward.

Using this schema, one can distinguish between the utilitarian and natural law interpretations of Burke. The second principle, which is the most generally accepted aspect of Burke's theory, explains why many authors consider Burke a utilitarian. To the extent that Burke is considered a utilitarian, Proposition 3, his politics of expediency, is also interpreted in a strict utilitarian sense. A utilitarian version of the politics of expediency ignores any overarching, unifying principle or system of ethics. The happiness of the people, in terms of their own individual desires, becomes the only touchstone for political policy.

In contrast to this view, Keynes recognizes in his 1904 essay that Burke holds all five propositions. Hence, he recognizes that Burke's political philosophy is based on ethics and possesses something like the logical structure sketched above. Less clearly, he also seems to *approve* of it, although not of Burke's theologically based view of natural law.[5] Nevertheless, because Keynes called Burke a political utilitarian and, at one point in the essay, refers to him as 'almost a Benthamite', it is necessary to determine what he meant by this characterization.

Key to Keynes's interpretation of Burke is his description of Burke's doctrine of expediency. In the natural law interpretation of Burke's philosophy, expediency means prudence and is opposed to the imposition of abstract principles. Political prudence means flexibility in the face of complex and diverse social conditions and, in the 1904 essay, Keynes seems to interpret Burke's doctrine of expediency in this way. That Keynes held this view will also be demonstrated through a consideration of his analysis of the Peace Conference.

Burke's view of government, guided rationally and expediently, presupposes the existence of leaders who embody the ancient civic virtues. Proposition 5 is thus central to Burke's entire logic. In his essay, Keynes quotes Burke's 'admirable' description of 'the whole duty of man', which gives the traits of the virtuous man of privilege. If it can be shown that this schemata also describes Keynes's political philosophy, we may have an important clue to Keynes's own ethics for, then, Keynes's consequentialist reasoning becomes part of a more comprehensive morality. Consequentialism should be seen as the application of science to ethical public policy decisions. However, rather than argue that actions which are rational (on egoist or utilitarian grounds) are ethical, Keynes would take the opposite view: what is ethical is rational; and the problem facing political leaders is how to promote ethical principles and the happiness of the people, given the exigencies of a particular situation.

The 1904 essay begins with a discussion of the ethical system upon which Burke's politics are based in which Keynes tries to dispel the prevalent utilitarian view that Burke was hostile to the application of all abstract principles to questions of morality and government. He stresses that, because Burke saw government as a means, he was antagonistic to those who maintained that there are certain universally and intrinsically desirable political ends. Keynes describes Burke's position thus: 'there is no universal end in politics except that of general happiness' (Keynes, 1904c, p. 6), yet emphasizes that Burke believed in universals in morality (Ibid., p. 7). According to Keynes, earlier writers had unduly stressed Burke's dislike for general principles: Morley, for instance, underrated

... the extent of Burke's belief in intrinsic and universal goods. Politically he may, without serious inaccuracy, be described as a utilitarian; for, with the exception of occasional lapse, he sets before himself the happiness of the community as the sole and ultimate end of government. But ethically he can in no wise claim to have anticipated his distinguished contemporary (Keynes, 1904c, p. 7).

According to Keynes, just as strong as Burke's view of government as means is his conviction that 'there are certain fixed "standards of rectitude", certain acts essentially right and wrong, certain states essentially good and bad, which we can recognise on introspection and at which we must aim' (Ibid., p. 8).

Keynes reiterates that while Burke held that, in politics, there were no specific acts which ought always to be performed, 'he was far from believing that there is nothing specific which is always good' (Ibid., p. 9). As evidence of the qualities he considered to be 'most excellent in his fellows', those 'essentially good' states known almost intuitively, Keynes quotes what he calls an 'admirable passage' on Burke's view of the 'whole duty of man':

> In the meantime we are born only to be men. We shall do enough if we form ourselves to be good ones. It is therefore our business carefully to cultivate in our minds, to rear to the most perfect vigour and maturity, every sort of generous and honest feeling, that belongs in our nature, to bring the dispositions that are lovely in private life into the service and conduct of the commonwealth; so to be patriots as not to forget we are gentlemen. To cultivate friendships, and to incur enmities. To have both strong, but both selected: in the one to be placable, in the other immovable. To model our principles to our duties and our situation. To be fully persuaded that all virtue which is impracticable is spurious; which leads us to act with effect and energy, than to loiter out our days without blame and without use (Keynes, 1904, pp. 9–10).

This passage constitutes a blueprint for members of the élite who are responsible for assuring good government. Keynes's approving citation suggests his understanding of the indispensable role of the civic virtues.

Clearly, Keynes recognized Burke's adherence to certain transcendental 'goods', but he notes that Burke's goods 'are all in the present; they do not involve any view of a "political millennium"'. He identifies religion as the foundation of civil society in Burke, 'and the source of all good, and of all comfort' (Keynes, 1904c, Section VIII). Moreover, he speaks of Burke's 'reverence' for private property as 'sacred, sacrosanct, the very ark of the covenant of society itself' (Ibid., p. 85, Section III).

Keynes did not consider Burke an ethical utilitarian – that is, one who holds that all moral acts are based on the principle of utility. Even in his discussion of Burke's goals of government he argues that it is hard to place Burke in any one school of political thought and comments that he is 'almost a Benthamite, often an intuitionist'. 'But', says Keynes, 'it is as one of the earliest exponents of *Laisser Faire*, of a modified political utilitarianism, and of expediency against abstract right, that he is most important in the history of opinion'.

> The ultimate and general end of government is, he declares, the happiness of the people as a whole. But certain restrictions upon the above are to be observed; not *all* the instruments of general happiness are within the competence of government, not only are the kinds of means that it can usefully employ limited, but the subsidiary ends conducive to general happiness, which it ought to seek, are themselves confined to certain types. He sometimes adds that ... equity, as well as utility, is an ultimate object. By equity he seems to mean an absence of artificial discrimination in respect to individuals or to classes, and he holds that such equity must never be overriden, even for purposes of apparent utility (Keynes, 1904c, Section III).

Keynes calls Burke a political utilitarian because, in politics, the end of government actions – when not overriden by questions of equity – is the happiness of the people. This is a *modified* political utilitarianism, because of his definition of happiness, and because of his overriding concern for equity in terms of 'moral equality' – the preservation of the 'natural' stations in life and the 'absence of artificial discrimination in respect to individuals', particularly the lack of any form of redistribution of income or property. The function of government is to oversee the pursuit of happiness and justice in these terms. The purpose of *laissez-faire* is thus to protect 'moral equality'.[6]

But Keynes also states that, ethically, Burke in no way anticipated Bentham (Keynes, 1904c, p. 7). Again, at the end of the essay, he repeats that Burke never held to the 'abstract' doctrines of utilitarianism 'save by fits and starts' (Ibid., p. 81) . Not only did he believe in a God-given hierarchy of values, he also believed in universal principles of morality: 'But out of physical causes unknown to us, perhaps unknowable, arise moral duties, which, as we are able perfectly to comprehend, we are bound indispensably to perform' (Ibid., p. 8). And he believed that excellence was defined in terms of virtue and the life of public participation. It was necessary to 'model our principles to our duties and our situation ... to act with effect and energy, than to loiter out our days without blame and without use' (Ibid., p. 10).

Related to this modified political utilitarianism is Burke's politics of expediency which Keynes describes as follows:

> ...in the maxims and precepts of the art of government expediency must reign supreme; whatever rights individuals may have, government has and

can have no right to do anything which is not for the general advantage (Keynes, 1904c, p. 36).

Keynes considered Burke's logical way of thinking about government to be his greatest contribution to politics. By distinguishing between the power to act and the moral right to use state power, he focused attention on establishing principles for good government which are principles of *moral* action. Keynes identified Burke as the first person to enunciate the doctrine of expediency clearly and consistently.

> It is expedient, he says, that government should have, in theory, sovereign powers, but it must never presume upon these powers; it is given the legal right to coerce, but it must never be sophistically deduced from this that it has the moral right to coerce whenever it will. We must never confuse 'can' with 'ought' (Keynes, 1904c, p. 37).

> It was a great discovery – this of Burke's.... to distinguish legal right from moral right, to put an end to the confusion between the power to act and the moral right to use this power, all this is the utmost importance for all clear and rational thinking on questions of government (Ibid., p. 81).

Peter J. Stanlis argues that misinterpretations about Burke's doctrine of expediency have arisen from a failure to understand the place of natural law in Burke's thought, and especially in his rejection of abstract rights. Morley and other utilitarian writers identified natural law with abstract speculation about the rights of man. Given Burke's objection to the latter, together with his views on government as a means, these writers concluded that Burke spurned the concept of natural law entirely, opting instead for a utilitarian politics of expediency. Stanlis points out that this view does a great disservice to Burke, for whom natural law was, in fact, a *sine qua non* of ethics, law and politics (Stanlis, 1958, p. 102).

In interpreting Burke's doctrine of expediency Keynes emphasizes Burke's objection to the arbitrary and imprudent use of power to impose unpopular measures on the citizenry. Through expedient use of power political leaders retain not only the power to coerce, but also the fundamental decisions about both ends and means. They increase their ability to exercise power if they rule wisely. The doctrine of expediency is used by political leaders to retain their power over public policy. Keynes recognizes that Burke did *not* mean that leaders should pander to the public's desires – a tendency which, for instance, he detested in Lloyd George's participation in the Treaty of Versailles.

As a means for promoting the happiness of the people, the doctrine of expediency can be seen as a substitute for that aspect of democratic government which assures a government *for* the people. However, according to both Burke and Keynes, it is a more effective means because it leads to more ethical, and therefore rational, results.

Keynes expressed ambivalence about Burke's views on the appropriate structure of political authority and the people's right to self-government. Although he approves of the logic of most of Burke's arguments against democratization, he nevertheless argues for some degree of mass political participation. Keynes agreed with Burke that the masses of people have no right to direct *self*-government, but that they only have a right to *good* government. Burke argued that it was dangerous for the people to be in a position to exert their 'transient will and uncertain judgement', although, they should have ultimate control over the ends of government. The extent of popular control was a matter of compromise: sometimes he argued that law must be based on the consent of the people and, sometimes, that the votes of the majority cannot alter the moral essence of things. Burke was quite clear, however, that the 'people' constituted only that limited number of males with adequate property and leisure to allow responsible thinking about public policy.

Keynes agrees that 'There is no very great *a priori* probability of arriving at desirable results by submitting to the decision of a vast body of persons, who are individually wholly incompetent to deliver a rational judgement on the affair at issue' (Keynes, 1904c, p. 57). However, he argues that democracy has worked reasonably well, while Burke's system of benevolent oligarchy has not. Furthermore, Keynes objects to vesting power in a 'representative class' of disinterested property-holders who are the 'natural representatives of the people', believing that no such class exists. Finally, he argues that Burke did not recognize the 'moral value' of self-government: 'The temper, which Burke feared, may be better restrained and modified by a means of expression, than by confinement under an authority however well intentioned' (Ibid., p. 58). Democratic practice is useful in co-opting or better managing the common people or, to put it more benignly, participation will contribute to their moral development.

To summarize, Keynes clearly understood Burke to hold the five principles identified at the beginning of this section. Furthermore, he seems to have agreed with the first three, and at least some aspects of the fourth and fifth. In his 1904 essay, Keynes agreed with Burke's élitist pessimism about the capabilities of common people to make decisions in their own long-term interests. Elitism in Keynes is an important and conservative aspect of his idealist politics which has not been adequately recognized in the recent work on Keynes and Burke. Control of public affairs by virtuous people who accept the 'whole duty of man' is essential to impose order on an otherwise disorderly world. Clearly, Burke understood this, but, as will be shown below, so did Keynes, as evidenced in his later work.

Given Keynes's acceptance of the logic of Burke's political philosophy, one can argue that he had a broader view of morality than utilitarian consequentialism. He takes a definitely ethical, as opposed to utilitarian, stand about the importance of moral responsibility to society. Some people, by virtue of their education, privilege, native abilities and character have an obligation to lead. Furthermore, these leaders must embody the greatest goods. One of these virtues is moderation – prudence or expediency. In this interpretation, Keynes's consequentialism is part of an act deontological morality, or of a deontological ethics of virtue.[7]

There is evidence for this deeper morality in Keynes's Apostles essays. In an undated and untitled paper on Moorean ethics (Keynes, 1910), Keynes argued for the extension of the things which have intrinsic value (and which we therefore have an obligation to create) to include 'states of affairs' (in contrast to isolated states of mind). These states of affairs are organic unities such as justice, beauty, tragedy, virtue, harmony and consistency. He argued that '"the good", which is correlative to "ought"' should include these desirable states. Although Keynes illustrates these desirable states of affairs as part of friendship rather than as part of civic responsibility, he argues for the *intrinsic* desirability of these traits, *not* their desirability as means.

Later Evidence of Keynes's Application of Burkean Logic

In 'Have We a Panacea?', an undated Apostles paper, Keynes reaffirms his basic agreement with Burkean political theory, emphasizing both his acceptance of expedience over abstract right and his élitism. Second, he tries, unsuccessfully, to deal with the major drawback of this politics – how to compete politically with panaceas which appeal directly to the emotions of the masses – an issue which he had raised at the end of the Burke essay where he commented on Burke's limited goals for mankind and the absence of political ideals. He recognizes their power to mobilize people toward beneficial ends, as well as disaster:

It is those naked generalisations concerning liberty and tolerance and empire and abstract rights, which he rightly and reasonably exposes, which have procured most of the great advances in politics as well as the most notable disasters (Keynes, 1904c, pp. 85–6).[8]

In 'Have We a Panacea?', Keynes describes Burke as 'the first to voice the modern feeling of helplessness and the worthlessness of panaceas', emphasizing how little power we have over the future. He reiterates his acceptance of Burke's principle of prudence over abstract principles:

We cannot, in fact, set before ourselves anything more particular than the general welfare.... We are feeling our way step by step; we are not moulding our world into conformity with some preformed standard, some pattern that we have spun a priori from our inner consciousness. For my own part I cannot but think that we are right.

However, he raises the real practical dilemma faced by such prudent politicians, how to compete with the political Utopians: 'How are we to gather unto ourselves the necessary fire and flame if we have no charm or incantation?' He argues: 'We must think out each step by purely intellectual means; but how is intellect ever to hold its own against the force and fury of those who think they have a panacea?' In notes attached to this essay he comments that 'we can't preach popularly our intellectual remedies'.

Keynes's application of Burkean logic to practical politics can be illustrated using Keynes's most famous piece of political analysis. In *The Economic Consequences of the Peace* there are striking parallels between Burke's and Keynes's thought on international relations and the nature of statesmanship. More important is the disdain which he showed for abstract speculation. Keynes's analysis of *The Economic Consequences of the Peace* demonstrates why, for Keynes, such speculation was the antithesis of the principle of political prudence.

Indeed, *The Economic Consequences of the Peace* can be read as a passionate plea for such prudence (although he seldom uses the word) and as a lesson in the evils of metaphysical modes of thought in politics. His portrait of Wilson, in particular, is an object lesson in the shortcomings of a mind and temperament which were 'essentially theological', whose abstraction produced both blindness and a kind of intellectual paralysis – an inability to come to grips with concrete reality (Keynes, 1971, p. 26).

He had no plan, no scheme, no constructive ideas whatever for clothing with the flesh of life the commandments which he had thundered from the White House. He could have preached a sermon on any of them or have addressed a stately prayer to the Almighty for their fulfilment; but he could not frame their concrete application to the actual state of Europe (Keynes, 1971, p. 27).

This passage highlights the qualities which both Burke and Keynes saw as essential to the statesman and statesmanship, and indeed as the linchpin of international discourse – an unflinching concern with fact and practice, custom and wont, coupled with a forthright consideration of human nature. Both Keynes and Burke shared a horror of the Procrustean bed of abstract theory. The essence of politics, and especially international politics, is a genuine regard for the differences which have been wrought by history and circumstance.

The practice of the art of politics necessitates not only flexibility, but also courage. It is this quality, as much as flexibility of mind and policy, which Keynes often found lacking at Versailles. He speaks of Lloyd George's capitulation to popular sentiment, to the unreason of the mob which, in words that echo Burke, violates the most fundamental quality of statesmanship – an élite determination to judge situations dispassionately, issuing in measured and considered policy.

Moreover, one surmises that the treaty achieved in Paris would have been as troublesome to Burke as it was to Keynes. Indeed, passages from the former seem almost to adumbrate the spirit and arguments of the latter. Stanlis notes that Burke

...conceived conquest in time of war as an act securing not merely physical power over an enemy, but also dictating a profound moral responsibility upon the victorious state, compelling it, under threat of forfeiting its acquired sovereignty, to grant the defeated people 'an equitable government' based on Natural Law (Stanlis, 1958, p. 93).

We see, then, marked similarities between the two men's views on issues of international relations. That Keynes drew his views in this area directly from Burke is moot, and perhaps beside the point. What is of signal importance is the logic of politics common to both, which resulted in a remarkably similar outlook.

Modern Civilization and The Inadequacy of Burke's Conservatism

In the 1904 essay Keynes identifies and objects to several aspects of Burke's conservatism: his distrust of inquiry into the truth of the matter in questions of morality; the sanctity of property and the evil consequences issuing from redistributing income or wealth; his extremely limited definition of justice in terms of 'moral equality'; his timidity about social, constitutional and parliamentary reform; and his trust in a benevolent oligarchy of great families and commercial interests. Keynes notes that these attitudes are buttressed by Burke's ability to ignore the facts of the situation and his concomitant limited foresight about the possibilities for profound and positive change. Although Keynes does not explicitly make the connection, this accounts for a tendency which he does recognize in Burke: his limited faith in the power of ideas and in the prospects for melioration and, therefore, the limitations in his idealism.

Despite Keynes's objection to most of these elements of Burke's conservatism, he finds a considerable amount of truth in Burke's arguments. He continually refers to Burke's tendency to overstate a doctrine, pressing it further than it will bear and spoiling it. In fact, the core of Keynes's criticism lies in Burke's disregard for truth, and his distrust of people's ability to make the right moral judgement, except by following conventional morality. Keynes comments that Burke's 'disbelief in the value to morality of a true analysis into moral judgements, prejudices and motives ... led him to undervalue the importance of truth in general (Keynes, 1904c, p. 11).

An important example of Burke's disregard for facts, to which Keynes objects, is his extravagant defence of unequal distribution of wealth. In the 1904 essay he recognizes the logical merit in Burke's argument against measures to alleviate poverty: since the poor vastly outnumber the rich, any redistributive schemes cannot help the poor very much, but can greatly damage the rich. However, in his 1905 Apostles essay, 'Modern Civilisation', Keynes points to Burke's failure to recognize that the conflicting demands of property and humanity could be accommodated through economic growth (Keynes, 1905b). In this essay, Keynes identifies the fallacy in Burke's conservative disregard for both the progress and the qualitative effects on social organization inherent in economic development. In emphasizing the fact and importance of capitalist economic development, he not only refutes Burke's arguments against the possibility of melioration of poverty, but, more importantly, identifies the logical error inherent in Burke's view of duty as unchanging (Keynes, 1906).

To contrast his own view with Burke's, Keynes quotes Burke: 'We know that *we* have made no discoveries, and we think that no discoveries are to be made, in morality – nor many in the great principles of government, nor in the ideas of liberty.' Noting the profound changes then shaking the whole fabric of society and using Burke's doctrine of expediency against him, he seems to chastize Burke for being insufficiently Burkean. He says that, although our ultimate goods are eternal and unchanging, 'it is not by reference to these alone that our duty is determined. What we ought to do is a matter of circumstances; metaphysically we can give no rules.' Because the whole fabric of society is being shaken, 'the mould in which it is cast, the traditions and the prejudices by which it is supported, the duties it involves are passing away. *Our duties may be changing.'*

> The differences in kind are due to the differences in the scale of the social organism.... We use different contrivances to lift a letter and to lift an elephant. A change in scale may revolutionise our method. In social life *duty* is our method, and with a far reaching difference in organisation of social life duty will change (Keynes, 1904c).

Note that Keynes uses both natural law logic and a *materialist* analysis of social change. Although ultimate goods are eternal, what is *natural* in social relations changes with social development. And he recognizes the importance of material forces, commenting: 'It may be possible, a hundred years hence, to investigate ... the influence of railways on morality.' Far-reaching qualitative change requires a flexible approach to duty. Keynes believed that the profound changes brought about by economic development required flexible leadership. This mandates the recognition of duty as *method*, as a *process* of problem-solving, as opposed to unchanging obligations to perform particular acts.

Thus, in this early essay, Keynes develops the implications of Burke's principle of expediency to justify both a commitment to public duty and an approach which emphasizes personal judgement based on a process of continuous weighing of objectives against possibilities arising from a changing consciousness of circumstances. In correcting Burke's prejudice against truth-seeking, Burkean political logic becomes the basis for Keynes's liberal, élitist politics – an interventionist politics appropriate to a period of dynamic instability, capable of encouraging social progress toward a more civilized post-capitalist world.[9]

Burkean Characteristics of Keynes's Elitist Politics

Keynes rejected much of the *content* of Burke's conservative politics which were based on his religious convictions about the nature and limits of goodness, and his conservative sociology which emphasized how goodness develops slowly in a social order based on a hierarchy of ranks. However, he adapted Burke's political élitism, which flows from their shared political philosophy, as well as from their shared prejudices that the world is a complex unity, and that political equality is unnatural.[10]

The wellspring of Keynes's conservatism is his acceptance of Burkean logic which *necessitates* government controlled by an élite. Despite Burke's protestations, inherent in his theory is a specific structure of government – oligarchic or élitist rule. Accepting the logic means accepting this conservative aspect. For Keynes, commitment to truth – that is, to the pursuit of the greatest good – required political power to be in the hands of persons who know the truth and who have the skills to manage the polity in a manner consistent with these universal goods. Fitzgibbons makes this point by calling Keynes an 'elitist liberal' (Fitzgibbons, 1988, pp. 166, 182–3).

Idealist politics are usually élitist. Burke, for instance, had little faith in the common people whom he regarded as easily swayed and susceptible to demagogues. Keynes expressed similar views and, in economics, his emphasis on the psychological propensities of consumers and investors is one example. Another was his fear of working-class revolt. The following from *The Economic Consequences of the Peace* sounds very Burkean.

> [Events in Russia] are the signal to us of how in the final catastrophe the malady of the body passes over into malady of the mind. Economic privation proceeds by easy stages, and so long as men suffer it patiently the outside world cares little....life proceeds somehow, until the limit of human endurance is reached at last and counsels of despair and madness stir the sufferers from the lethargy which precedes the crisis. Then man shakes himself, and the bonds of custom are loosed. The power of ideas is sovereign, and he listens to whatever instruction of hope, illusion, or revenge is carried to him on the air (Keynes, 1971, pp. 158–9).

The 'people' are not usually a positive force in social change. The power of popular sentiment in democratic politics serves most often to pervert the legitimate ends and means of statesmanship.

Keynes's views on class politics in Britain's party system reverberate with his élitism. Indeed, Keynes's views on twentieth-century political parties parallel Burke's views on eighteenth-century political factions. Keynes argued for strong party discipline, for reliance on expert advice on technical matters, and for party leadership capable of understanding the views of the membership and of educating them. In 'Am I a Liberal?' he argues in favour of an autocratic party machine (Keynes, 1972a, pp. 295–6). In the same essay Keynes explained his preference for the Liberal Party because it was free of class bias and was therefore freer to chart a course of moderation and wisdom. The Conservative Party, among other faults, 'conforms to no intellectual standard – it is not even safe, or calculated to preserve from spoilers that degree of civilisation which we have already attained' (Keynes, 1972a, pp. 296–7). As for the Labour Party, he considered it impossible for the intellectuals to exercise adequate control, mainly because of the power of the left-wing extremist element 'which hates or despises existing institutions and believes that great good will result merely from overthrowing them' (Keynes, 1972a, p. 299).

Nevertheless, post-war changes in the economy mandated a new political coalition between the Liberals and Labour Party to facilitate a progressive shift away from *laissez-faire*. Application of Burkean political maxims is particularly obvious in Keynes's advocacy of this coalition. He considered the progressives in the Liberal Party as an independent brains trust for the Labour Party, almost a *faction* of Labour outside the Labour Party. In 'Liberalism and Labour', Keynes argues in Burkean terms for early implementation of progressive policies to avoid the dangers in waiting for Labour to win power on its own as a result of mounting mistakes by the Conservatives. Keynes feared that too long a delay might find the country confronted with extreme alternatives (a clear application of one of Burke's maxims of expediency). The 'socialist' elements of the Liberal Party would be the constructive, dispassionate dispensers of prudent ideas for the Labour Party. Because they are outside the Labour Party, they do not 'have to do lip-service to trade-unionist tyrannies, to the beauties of the class war, or to doctrinaire State Socialism' (Keynes, 1926, pp. 309–10).

CONCLUSIONS

This paper has demonstrated Burke's influence on Keynes's political philosophy. It has been shown that Burke was the source both of Keynes's liberal interventionist politics and his conservative élitism. Burke's ethical theory of the state, when separated from his conservative scepticism about the possibilities for human progress and his inadequate appreciation of the facts, provides the strategy for an activist liberal, but élitist, politics:

1. Politics must be based on ethical presuppositions about the good.
2. Government must be seen as a means to promote the general happiness, *not* the interest of specific groups.
3. Political power should reside in an élite of disinterested leaders who are embodiments of the greatest goods.
4. Practical politics must be based on the principle of expediency rather than abstract principles, steering a course between immediate desires and what is ethical.
5. In politics, the principle of utility should never override justice.

Keynes identified the major source of Burke's conservatism, in his undervaluation of truth and therefore his inadequate understanding of the impact of capitalist economic development on both the nature of public duty and the possibilities for a just and humane society. Keynes created his twentieth-century liberal politics by reasserting the pre-eminence of truth-seeking, or more accurately perhaps, of practical rationality based on Keynes's view of probability.[11] He condemned Burke's exaggeration, his excesses and his often myopic interpretations of reality; but he retained an essential conservative ingredient of Burke's politics – his élitism.[12]

This paper also touches on an important underlying similarity in world-view which is the basis for Keynes's and Burke's objections to abstract principles. Both men saw social life as a complex, inherently imperfect, constantly changing totality. This shared world-view explains their similar approaches to theory construction and its use in the political process. For Burke, viewing society as an organic unity did not imply an orderly system. He assumed chaotic reaction to imposed change based on abstract principles which impute too much rationality to people. The 'natural' (God-given, historically evolved) hierarchical social order of classes and the moral order provided through 'just prejudice' represent rationality in the system. This rationality, immanent in the system as a whole, implies slow evolution, but the connections between past, present and future are so intricate and mysterious that one must proceed with reform with extreme care.

Keynes basically shared Burke's metaphysical view of society as an organic unity. However, he had a more optimistic, secular, and materialist view of the possibilities for progress. He had witnessed tumultuous economic, social and political change and recognized that such fast-moving qualitative developments required an activist policy stance. In turn, this activism required a theoretical approach to understanding the economy which combines science and art and recognizes economics as a moral science which guides public policy. This is an application of Keynes's comment that 'in social life duty is *method*'.

Burke's and Keynes's pragmatism follows from this world-view. Thus Burke may have been an important early influence on Keynes's views both of political and scientific practice. Burke's distaste for abstract theorizing, his unwillingness to think in terms of universals, the importance he attached to designing policy which recognizes the particular circumstances of a situation are all components of Keynes's methodology.[13]

This interpretation of Burke and Keynes also has implications for Keynes's ethics. It explains the sense in which Keynes considered Burke (and presumably himself) a political, but not an ethical, utilitarian. In politics there are ends to be achieved, and specific goals which can be articulated. However, both Keynes and Burke recognized that, even in achieving fairly clear goals, the process is not usually mechanical. In his early essays on Burke, Keynes clearly indicates his own rejection of the hedonist utilitarianism based on rational egoism which underlies both classical and neoclassical economics. Furthermore, he follows Burke in rejecting reductionist analysis of consequences based on a calculus of expected costs and benefits, which, in a sense, is just one manifestation of applying abstract analysis to practical affairs.

Clearly, Burke took a stronger ethical point of view than that contained in utilitarianism and neoclassical economics. He assumed the existence of both universal goods and duties, that justice should always override utility, and an ethics of virtue – namely, that leaders should embody the greatest goods. Keynes, too, seems to adopt this ethical position, but in his early work on probability he developed a different understanding of what the performance of duty entails, an elaboration of his view in 'Modern Civilisation' that, in social life, duty is one's method. He worked out a guide to practice which gives human judgement a much greater role than implied in Burke's statements about the universality of duty. According to this interpretation, the *Treatise on Probability* is crucial to understanding Keynes's ethics and his view of economics as a moral science.

This paper suggests that Burke provided an early inspiration for Keynes. Further work on the Burke–Keynes connection should provide more insight into Keynes, and, more importantly, to the ethical dimension of economics.

NOTES

1   I wish to acknowledge the help of Judith Allan who made the Keynes manuscripts available to me at the Marshall Library in Cambridge, as well as Dr. Michael Halls for his help with the Keynes papers in the Modern Archives at King's College Library. Permission to quote from unpublished manuscripts in the J.M. Keynes Papers in King's College Library was kindly granted by King's College, Cambridge University. Unpublished writings of J.M. Keynes © The Provost and Scholars of King's College, Cambridge, 1990. In addition, I have benefited greatly from discussions and critique of this and related work by Robert Skidelsky, Rod O'Donnell and Athol Fitzgibbons. Finally, I am deeply indebted to Bruce Watson for his research and editorial aid in writing this paper as well as discussions about it.

2.   The Apostles papers are a series of short essays that Keynes delivered, mainly as an undergraduate, before the secret and select discussion group known as the Apostles. The group often focused its Saturday night discussions on questions about how one should live one's life. After G. E. Moore's *Principia Ethica* was published in 1903, they spent many evenings discussing the ethical issues raised by Moore. But Keynes's papers also considered questions raised through his study of Burke. These papers, the 1904 essay on Burke, and miscellaneous papers and notes, are housed in the Modern Archives, King's College Library. I have relied on dating for two undated papers supplied by O'Donnell (1989a, p. 385).

3.   See Fitzgibbons, 1988, p. 72, endnote 1.

4.   O'Donnell calls Keynes a political rationalist, *not* in the epistemological sense that Keynes held certain abstract political principles to be self-evidently true, but in 'the looser sense of conceiving the essence of politics to be persuasive appeals to reason' (O'Donnell, 1989a, p. 276). However, because he considers Burke a utilitarian, O'Donnell considers G. E. Moore rather than Burke the major influence on Keynes's political philosophy.

5.   An important question is the extent of Keynes's acceptance of any version of natural law. Both O'Donnell and Carabelli argue against a natural law interpretation, at least in his acceptance of the existence of natural duties. However, Keynes did recognize the existence of universals in goodness and a natural hierarchy of the greatest goods, so one can argue Keynes's acceptance of this aspect of natural human characteristics.

6.   Keynes's use of the term political utilitarianism to describe Burke is something

of a misnomer, giving the false impression that Burke presaged such schools as modern public choice theory. To repeat, the term is meant to convey the idea that the purpose of government is to promote the happiness of the people.

7. The question of Keynes's consequentialism is also controversial. Skidelsky considers Keynes a utilitarian; and O'Donnell calls Keynes's philosophy of practical reason developed in the *Treatise on Probability* a probabilistic form of act-consequentialism (O'Donnell, 1989a, p. 116). However, Fitzgibbons argues convincingly that Keynes did not agree that doing good should take precedence over being good; that is, he disagreed with Bentham's criteria of 'social utility', of one's obligation to promote the greatest good for the greatest number regardless of the effect on the individual (Fitzgibbons, 1988, p. 168). Second, he quotes Keynes's statements to the effect that the Benthamite calculus represents 'false calculation', because 'the hypothesis of a calculable future leads to a wrong interpretation of the principles of behaviour which the need for action compels us to adopt' (Fitzgibbons, 1988, p. 95). Carabelli also rejects the consequentialist interpretation, contending that in the *Treatise on Probability* Keynes argued that rationality is ordinarily based on probability 'grounded on ordinary practice and therefore to be approached by the tools of ordinary language and everyday qualitative and analogical reasoning, rather than by formal and artificial language and by purely quantitative, mathematical tools' (Carabelli, 1988, p. 234).

8. Compare this quote with the final paragraph of *The General Theory:* 'the ideas of economists and political philosophers, both when they are right and when they are wrong, are more powerful than is commonly understood. Indeed the world is ruled by little else.... I am sure that the power of vested interests is vastly exaggerated compared with the gradual encroachment of ideas.... it is ideas, not vested interests, which are dangerous for good or evil' (Keynes, 1964, p. 383–4).

9. In making this argument I disagree with Skidelsky's conclusion that Keynes, as a follower of Moore, never developed a logical justification for pursuing public duty. Skidelsky argues that Moore failed to provide a complete ethical system. Moore rejected the hedonist definition of good in favour of his own idealist values; he disconnected ethics from social utility and conventional morality, and he did not show how to relate his goods to the practical business of life. Neither did he show how to harmonize the private and public spheres – the good life and the useful life. Skidelsky argues for a strong strain of egoism in Keynes. According to this interpretation, as a Moorite, Keynes was not obliged to pursue political and social goals; however, they 'could be given Moorite justification under certain circumstances – when, for example the ordered existence of society, which was the ultimate condition of the possibility of good states of mind, was threatened' (Skidelsky, 1983, p. 154). O'Donnell disagrees with Skidelsky, but because he discounts Burke's influence on Keynes, he tries, unsuccessfully in my view, to maintain that Keynes developed an adequate justification for obligation to public life from Moore (O'Donnell, 1989a, p. 276).

10. For Burke, social, economic *and* political inequality was natural, because of the hierarchical nature of the social order. For Keynes, inequality was natural because of genetically (and possibly environmentally) determined individual differences.

11. Anna Carabelli argues convincingly that it was not 'truth' that Keynes was after, at least in his analysis of social life, but reasonableness or rationality. His goal was to apply reason to public policy issues, recognizing the probabilistic nature of our knowledge. She argues that Keynes viewed rationality as 'practical and continent, utterly separated from truth and relative to actual limited cognitive conditions' of the policy maker (Carabelli, 1988, p. 234). This seems a more accurate interpretation of Keynes's approach to economics and public policy formation. However,

as a Moorite, truth remained important in his ethics, for throughout his life he continued to recognize the ideals as ultimate ends of human life.

12.   Many would question the validity of this élitist view. But it is even more problematic today, given the increased importance of accommodating to mass public opinion.

13.   See Anna Carabelli (1988) *On Keynes's Method.*

4. The Rules of the Road: Keynes's Theoretical Rationale for Public Policy

Bradley W. Bateman

The traditional subject of the debates about 'what Keynes really meant' has been his theoretical work. By 1962, twenty-five years after *The General Theory* was published, there was an emerging agreement that Keynes was 'about' wage rigidity and liquidity traps; but this consensus was quickly unravelled in 1968 with the publication of Axel Leijonhuvud's *On Keynesian Economics and the Economics of Keynes*. Since then, we have been offered so many interpretations of Keynes's theoretical apparatus that it is probably not even proper to speak of a debate. Because there are now so many mutually exclusive descriptions of Keynes it is perhaps more correct to characterize Keynesian scholarship as a noisy dining hall filled with the din of conversations coming from many tables. We now have several discussions rather than one debate.

With time, this din has been deepened with several new sounds. G.L.S. Shackle's work in the early 1960s reminded economists that Keynes had been interested in uncertainty throughout his life, but that this had been ignored in virtually all interpretations of his thinking. This partly spilled over into conversations about Keynes's theoretical work, but it has also spawned several new types of discussions, the first of which concerns method. The concern with uncertainty points to Keynes's early *Treatise on Probability* and to the broader questions of how one models expectations. Set in the broader context of the rational expectations revolution, this discussion quickly evolved into a full and mature consideration of Keynes's methodology.[1]

This concern with methodology has, in turn, pointed the way to a second new type of discussion about the importance of Keynes's philosophical work to his economics. Readers who turned to *Probability* quickly realized that it was merely the outcropping of several deeper philosophical concerns: epistemology, ethics, natural law, chance and

55

causality. This clearly pointed to the need for a fuller understanding of the influences on Keynes's early thinking, and several scholars have begun to examine his early, unpublished Cambridge essays which deal extensively with his broader philosophical concerns (for example, 'Ethics in Relation to Conduct', 'Egoism', 'Beauty').[2]

This paper might be a part of several of these discussions, since it is partly grounded in this most recent conversation about the philosophical influences on Keynes's thought, examining in particular the rationale for Keynes's policy proposals. The crux of the discussion, however, is purely theoretical and hence falls into the older tradition of standard doctrine histories. Keynes was concerned from his earliest philosophical writings to his final economic theorizing with mathematical expectation or what we now call the expected utility model. The vehicle for this paper's argument is Keynes's changing conception of mathematical expectation. Although this, in turn, has certain broad implications regarding his methodology, apart from indicating these implications, this paper is necessarily not concerned with method. The real point is to make a particular connection between theory and ethics.

OBJECTIVE EXPECTATION[3]

The story of Keynes's concern with ethics and analysis begins with his arrival at Cambridge in 1902. Being from a well-known Cambridge family and having already demonstrated exceptional abilities, Keynes was almost immediately vetted by the Cambridge Conversazione Society, better known as the Apostles, which met on Saturday evenings to discuss a paper read by one of its members. Keynes had the particular good fortune to have been elected to membership at the time that the philosopher G. E. Moore was gaining prominence, and the papers often dealt with issues and topics suggested by Moore's writings.

One of these which particularly concerned Keynes and the younger Apostles was the role of rules in right conduct. Moore's *Principia Ethica,* published in 1903, advocated the need for following rules in certain circumstances, but this made several of the younger Apostles uneasy. Although they clearly considered themselves disciples of Moore, especially in his rejection of utilitarianism, they were very much a part of the Edwardian age and firmly rejected the need for rules.

Keynes accepted the challenge that this posed and attempted to resolve the issue by extending the argument that Moore used against utilitarianism to make a broader case against rules.

Moore's rejection of utilitarianism was based on an argument that what is good is not necessarily synonymous with what is useful or desired. Moore took traditional utilitarianism to argue for the supremacy of individual desires in ethical matters – that is, that the basis for making an ethical decision should be the utility which individuals will experience as a result of the decision. In his commonsense fashion, Moore rejected this argument by pointing out that the things which give people utility and which they desire are often very bad. Moore did not deny that a thing could be both desired and good; he merely denied that all desired things are also good things.

Arguing in this fashion, Moore asserted that good is a fundamental concept irreducible to any other definition. Good is good: it is not necessarily anything else such as the desired, the natural, the divine or the inevitable. 'If I am asked "What is good?" my answer is that good is good, and that is the end of the matter' (Moore, 1903, p. 6). He believed that people generally understand the unique nature of good and his point was merely to disabuse them of the ideas put forward by ethical theorists espousing various misconceptions. Moore took good to be an objective quality which we recognize in things and argued that ethically correct decisions consist of recognizing this quality and acting in such as way as to cause the largest possible amount of it to exist.

This much of Moore's argument was enthusiastically embraced by the Apostles. They wanted a good world and believed that it was achieved through the correct identification of good things. The pursuit of friendship, truth and beauty was to be greatly preferred to the pursuit of money or other 'useful' things. The point of their departure from Moore regarded how to attain the good.

In cases in which the outcomes of one's actions were certain, the only ethical problem for Moore involved identifying the outcome which resulted in the most good. When one was uncertain about the outcome of one's action, however, Moore argued that one was obliged to follow general rules of conduct. His argument is a probabilistic one, based on mathematical expectation. 'We have, however, not only to consider the relative goodness of different effects, but also the relative probability of their being obtained' (Ibid., p. 166). Using this logic, he argued that the general rules of conduct represent those with the highest expected value or that breaking these rules represents an option with low probability of good results.

It seems, then, that with regard to any rule which is *generally* useful, we may assert that it ought *always* to be observed, not on the ground that in *every* particular case it will be useful, but on the ground that in *any* particular case the probability of its being so is greater than that of our being likely to decide rightly that we have before us an instance of its disutility. In short, though we may be sure that there are cases where the rule should be broken, we can never know which those cases are, and ought, therefore, never to break it (Moore, 1903, pp. 162–3, emphasis in original).

Keynes made his analytical departure from Moore on this point. 'The large part played by considerations of probability in his theory of right conduct was, indeed, an important contributory cause to my spending all the leisure of many years on the study of that subject (*CW*, x, p. 445). Keynes correctly perceived that Moore's argument depended on a frequency theory of probability and began to work on an alternative in several of his early Apostles papers. His ideas were further developed in his Prize Fellowship essays (the unsuccessful 1907 version and its revision in 1908) and took its final form in *A Treatise on Probability*.[4]

The result was his argument that probabilities are objective degrees of belief rather than relative frequencies. The frequency with which things occur may influence our degrees of belief, Keynes argued, but these are two fundamentally different things.

> Let our premises consist of any set of propositions *h*, and our conclusion consist of any set of propositions *a*, then, if a knowledge of *h* justifies a rational belief in *a* of degree α, we say that there is a *probability-relation* of degree α between *a* and *h*.
>
> In ordinary speech we often describe the conclusion as being doubtful, uncertain, or only probable. But, strictly, these terms ought to be applied, either to the degree of our *rational belief* in the conclusion, or to the relation or argument between two sets of propositions, knowledge of which would afford grounds for a corresponding degree of rational belief (*CW*, VIII, pp. 4–5).

Furthermore, Keynes asserted, these degrees of belief are objective and 'not ... subject to human caprice'.

> But in the sense important to logic, probability is not subjective. It is not, that is to say, subject to human caprice. A proposition is not probable because we think it so. When once the facts are given which determine our knowledge, what is probable or improbable in these circumstances has been fixed objectively, and is independent of our opinion. The theory of probability is logical, therefore, because it is concerned with the degree of belief which it is *rational* to entertain in given conditions, and not merely with the actual beliefs of particular individuals, which may or may not be rational (Ibid., p. 4).

These objective degrees of belief obviated the need to follow rules by eliminating the frequency of outcomes as an explicit part of the calculation of correct behaviour. In Moore's argument, it was the long-run average outcome which dictated correct behaviour: because one does not have omniscience regarding the times when a better outcome would result from violating the rule, one is obliged to follow the rule and guarantee the highest possible proportion of good outcomes. In Keynes's argument, the long-run average has no direct relevance; a person weighs each outcome of an action by her degree of belief in its occurrence and chooses the action which she believes will yield the greatest good. By weighing objectively knowable good by objectively knowable probability, each person is capable of evaluating a situation for herself. The objective expectation of the good produced by alternative actions frees one from the need to blindly follow rules.

SUBJECTIVE EXPECTATION[5]

For many, the discourse above might seem to be all that is necessary for an understanding of Keynes's rationale for economic policy. In economists' standard formulations there are two approaches to policy: following rules and exercising discretion. In this simple dichotomy, Keynes is normally cast against the monetarists or the rational expectationists as the founder and chief proponent of exercising discretion in policy. In this view, a coherent story explaining Keynes's early rejection of rules would be a sufficient explanation of the ethical and analytical bases for his position.

In fact, however, the story is much more complicated than this. Although it is true that Keynes was opposed to the rigid adherence to policy rules, he was eventually to come to the position that some types of rules are important.[6] In addition, he was to eventually jettison the analytical bases for his rejection of rules: objective good and objective probability. The completion of the story thus requires an explanation of these analytical changes, as well as the role of these changes in his belief that general rules of conduct are necessary.

The first part of Keynes's objective expectations to be explicitly abandoned was the concept of objective probabilities. Appropriately enough, this came in response to the criticism of an Apostle of a later generation, Frank Ramsey. Ramsey had published a highly critical review of *Probability* in 1922 in *The Cambridge Review* to which Keynes made no published response; but when Ramsey's constructive alternative to Keynes's theory was published posthumously in 1931, Keynes graciously conceded defeat.

The essence of Ramsey's criticism was to deny that there was an objective basis for Keynes's degrees of belief.

> ... a ... fundamental criticism of Mr. Keynes' views, is the obvious one that there really do not seem to be any such things as the probability relations he describes. He supposes that, at any rate in certain cases, they can be perceived; but speaking for myself I feel confident that this is not true. I do not perceive them, and if I am to be persuaded that they exist it must be by argument; moreover I shrewdly suspect that others do not perceive them either, because they are able to come to so very little agreement as to which of them relates any two given propositions (Ramsey, 1931, p. 161).

Whereas Keynes had argued that one's degree of belief is dependent on a correctly intuited logical relationship, Ramsey argued that degrees of belief are subjective and nothing more than a reflection of a person's beliefs.

> In order therefore to construct a theory of quantities of belief which shall be both general and more exact, I propose to take as a basis a general psychological theory, which is now universally discarded, but nevertheless comes, I think, fairly close to the truth in the sort of cases with which we are most concerned. I mean the theory that we act in the way we think most likely to realize the objects of our desires, so that a person's actions are completely determined by his desires and opinions (Ibid., p. 173).

Keynes ceded the point to Ramsey.

> Ramsey argues, as against the view which I put forward, that probability is concerned not with objective relations between propositions but (in some sense) with degrees of belief, and he succeeds in showing that the calculus of probabilities simply amounts to a set of rules for ensuring that the system of degrees of belief which we hold shall be a consistent system. Thus the calculus of probabilities belongs to formal logic. But the basis of our degrees of belief– or the *a priori* probabilities, as they used to be called – is part of our human outfit, perhaps given us merely by natural selection, analogous to our perceptions and our memories rather than to formal logic. So far I yield to Ramsey – I think he is right (*CW*, X, pp. 338–9).

Interestingly, however, Keynes made no reference in his review to another analytical novelty in Ramsey's treatment of expectation. In order to measure subjective probabilities, Ramsey had offered a schema based on mathematical expectation, or what we call today the expected utility model. In prefacing the technical aspects of his schema, he carefully distanced the 'utilities' used in his calculations from any ethical considerations. 'It should be emphasized that in this essay good and bad are never to be understood in any ethical sense but simply as denoting that to which a given person feels desire and aversion' (Ramsey, 1931, p. 174).

This use of purely hedonistic preference was as far removed from Moore's objective good as subjective degrees of belief were from Keynes's objective probabilities. But although he made no reference to this other contrast in his review of Ramsey, we know that Keynes did eventually forsake his belief in an objective Moorean good. The only question is *when* he changed his mind.

His abandonment is first reported in 'My Early Beliefs', an autobiographical essay presented in 1938 to the Memoir Club in order to help second-generation Bloomsburies better understand the influence of Moore and *Principia Ethica* on the first generation. In the essay, he is trying both to explain the beliefs of the pre-war Apostles and to point out the fallacies involved in these beliefs. Thus, he gently chides himself and his brothers for their 'neo-platonism' in their attempts to discern the good in their 'timeless, passionate states of contemplation and communion'.

> How did we know what states of mind were good? This was a matter of direct inspection, of direct unanalysable intuition about which it was useless and impossible to argue.
> I have called this faith a religion, and some sort of relation of neo-platonism it surely was. But we should have been very angry at the time with such a suggestion. We regarded all this as entirely rational and scientific in character (*CW*, IX, pp. 437–8).

But, for all the virtue he saw in growing up in this heady ether, he was forced to conclude that 'it was hardly a state of mind which a grown-up person in his senses could sustain literally'.

The only question remaining, then, is when Keynes experienced his change of heart about the existence of objective good. But while this is an important question in the history of ideas, it is enough for our purposes to be able to answer that it must have happened sometime prior to the 1930s. Keynes was 54 when he wrote 'My Early Beliefs' in 1938, and we can be sure that he was not referring to a recent change of opinion.

THE NEED FOR RULES

Thus, while we do not know the exact dates of Keynes's changes of heart regarding objective good and objective probability, we can be sure that they had occurred by the time he had begun working on *The General Theory* in 1931. And it is there, in his final theoretical work, that the *consequences* of his changed beliefs are most evident. For, although *The General Theory* has traditionally been thought of as an argument for discretionary policy, it is so in only a very limited sense. Many commentators have pointed out, for instance, that there is very little (almost no) mention of fiscal policy in the book which is most commonly associated with the idea of using government deficits to stimulate the economy. Peden (1988), Kahn (1984), Meltzer (1989), and Moggridge and Howson (1974), for instance, have all pointed to the lack of any general concern with fiscal policy in *The General Theory*.

The point, of course, is not that Keynes was against the use of monetary or fiscal policy altogether. This was clearly not the case. But it is the case that *The General Theory* provides scant and tepid enthusiasm for fiscal policy. Likewise, it is well documented that Keynes never publicly supported debt-financed public expenditure after the early 1930s and that, by 1937, he was calling for fiscal restraint. The point, rather, is to explain the *analytical basis* for Keynes's limited enthusiasm for discretionary policy and to provide a clearer understanding of his concern with rules.[7]

To clarify Keynes's case for rules, it is probably easiest to return to 'My Early Beliefs' and the story of his abandoning an objective conception of good.[8] After explaining his inability to sustain his neo-Platonic beliefs, Keynes goes on to explain that his early beliefs involved another 'flimsily based' fallacy.

> We were among the last of the Utopians, or meliorists as they are sometimes called, who believe in a continuing moral progress by virtue of which the human race already consists of reliable, rational, decent people, influenced by truth and objective standards ...(*CW*, X, p. 447).

It was, thus, not only the belief that good is an objective quality, but also the belief that people pursued it which marked Keynes's youthful thought.

> I have said that we were amongst the first to escape from Benthamism. But another eighteenth-century heresy we were the unrepentant heirs and last upholders. We were among the last of the Utopians, or meliorists as they are

sometimes called, who believe in a continuing moral progress by virtue of which the human race already consists of reliable, rational, decent people, influenced by truth and objective standards, who can be safely released from the outward restraints of convention and traditional standards and inflexible rules of conduct, and left, from now onwards, to their own sensible devices, pure motives and reliable intuitions of the good. As cause and consequence of our general state of mind we completely misunderstood human nature, including our own. The rationality which we attributed to it led to a superficiality, not only of judgement, but also of feeling (*CW*, X, pp. 447–8).

The analytical ramifications of this are clear. Whereas the youthful Keynes would have had 'reliable, rational' people willingly contemplating the good that would result from their actions and the degree to which they could believe this good would occur, the mature Keynes was left with people pursuing a plethora of ends (good, bad, and otherwise) and employing subjective degrees of belief regarding the likelihood of their outcomes. The young Keynes had not needed rules because people were 'rational' and sought what was 'truly' good; the mature Keynes needed rules because people were 'irrational' and acted from a multitude of motivations.

The rules Keynes envisioned, however, were not simply moral strictures against 'bad' behaviour. Indeed, he acknowledged that some feelings associated with wickedness were valuable. The real role of rules lay in the realm of probabilities.

This is most obvious in the analytical structure of *The General Theory*. Keynes uses mathematical expectation both to construct his model of macroeconomic (read general) equilibrium and to explain the fluctuations in that equilibrium. Although expectation plays a formal part in the construction of aggregate demand, aggregate supply, the propensity to consume, liquidity preference and the marginal efficiency of capital, it is in these last two that Keynes focuses his concern.

The importance of expectations to liquidity preference is straightforward, although it was largely overlooked for some 25 years. The amount of cash which people hold for speculative purposes is determined, in part, by their expectations of future interest rates. If one takes the primary determinant to be correct interest rates, this means that expected interest rates are a *ceteris paribus* condition of the liquidity preference function.

In dealing with the speculative-motive it is, however, important to distinguish between the changes in the rate of interest which are due to changes in the supply of money available to satisfy the speculative-motive, without there having been any change in the liquidity function, and those which are primarily due to changes in expectation affecting the liquidity function itself. Open-market operations may, indeed, influence the rate of interest through both channels, since they may not only change the volume of money, but may also give rise to changed expectations concerning the future policy of the Central Bank or of the Government. Changes in the liquidity function itself, due to a change in the news which causes revision of expectations, will often be discontinuous, and will, therefore, give rise to a corresponding discontinuity of change in the rate of interest (*CW*, VII, pp. 197–8).

The importance of this for Keynes lies in the implications for monetary policy.

Since people use subjective probabilities in forming their expectations of future interest rates, they are liable to hold so much money in times of high uncertainty that cash will be relatively scarce and current interest rates too high to achieve full employment. This is a particularly vexing problem since the subjective probabilities of the speculators are, by definition, not susceptible to easy manipulation. Monetary authorities can make any amount of money available, but if people have ever larger cash holdings, then current rates will not go down.

Thus a monetary policy which strikes public opinion as being experimental in character or easily liable to change may fail in its objective of greatly reducing the long-term rate of interest, because M_2 may tend to increase almost without limit in response to a reduction of r below a certain figure. The same policy, on the other hand, may prove easily successful if it appeals to public opinion as being reasonable and practicable and in the public interest, rooted in strong conviction, and promoted by an authority unlikely to be superseded (Ibid., p. 203).

The clear implication is that discretionary policy has very narrow limits for effectiveness. It must be noted, however, that the problem for Keynes is not a plethora of individual expectations concerning the future interest rate. Although people use subjective probabilities in forming their expectations, they also have a tendency to seek out and employ the conventional belief as to what the future holds.

It might be more accurate, perhaps, to say that the rate of interest is a highly conventional, rather than a highly psychological, phenomenon. For its actual value is largely governed by the prevailing view as to what its value is expected to be. *Any* level of interest which is accepted with sufficient con-viction as *likely* to be durable *will* be durable; subject, of course, in a changing society to fluctuations for all kinds of reasons round the expected normal. In particular, when M_1 is increasing faster than M, the rate of interest will rise, and *vice versa*. But it may fluctuate for decades about a level which is chronically too high for full employment (Ibid., pp. 203–4).

Clearly, then, the right kind of monetary policy is one which convinces speculators of low future rates and thereby establishes a new *convention* amongst them. Given the nature of speculator expectations, a good monetary policy is one which is *not* regularly changing and supports a conventional interpretation of low long-term interest rates.

The nature of this policy dilemma is even more prominent in the investment demand function. In describing the nature of the expectations which influence investment, Keynes employs an even more extensive explanation of how subjective probabilities are influenced by the conventional interpretation of what the future holds.

> How then are these highly significant daily, even hourly, revaluations of existing investments carried out in practice?
>
> In practice we have tacitly agreed, as a rule, to fall back on what is, in truth, a *convention*. The essence of this convention – though it does not, of course, work out quite so simply – lies in assuming that the existing state of affairs will continue indefinitely, except in so far as we have specific reasons to expect a change. This does not mean that we really believe that the existing state of affairs will continue indefinitely. We know from extensive experience that this is most unlikely. The actual results of an investment over a long term of years very seldom agree with the initial expectation.... We are assuming, in effect, that the existing market valuation, however arrived at, is uniquely correct in relation to our existing knowledge of the facts which will influence the yield of the investment, and that it will only change in proportion to changes in this knowledge... (Ibid., pp. 151–2).

This poses a significant policy problem in that Keynes believed that fluctuations in investment demand are the primary cause of the business cycle.

> I suggest that the essential character of the Trade Cycle and, especially, the regularity of time sequence and of duration which justifies calling it a cycle, is mainly due to the way in which the marginal efficiency of capital fluctuates (Ibid., p. 313).

If the end of policy is to dampen or alleviate the business cycle, then the means to that end must be the establishment of a conventional expectation of high profits to maintain high levels of current investment.

Thus, the problem for policy-makers is a very subtle one. They must understand and use monetary and fiscal policy to control the business cycle, but they are constrained by the expectations of speculators, entrepreneurs, and business managers. Policy which is too irregular or too sporadic may cause high cash holdings and low levels of investment. Policy-makers are constrained to work within a relatively narrow range in order to maintain the conventionally determined expectations that control the economy. The subjectivity of expectations means a constrained policy is necessary to maintain a conventional belief in stability and growth.[9]

THE RHETORIC OF RULES

The most difficult barrier to understanding Keynes's argument for rules is undoubtedly rhetorical. Whereas rules today are generally taken to be of the form of a fixed percentage growth rate for the money supply or a balanced budget, Keynes envisioned something less restrictive than this. He could not be classed with the adherents of either of these schools of strict rules.

Yet he clearly believed that rules were necessary and that policy-makers properly worked within narrow bounds. In changing from a belief in objective expectation to a belief in subjective expectation he saw a need to control unruly investors and speculators; and this would come about only through policies which instilled confidence in their own stability. The conventions which are followed in forming expectations had to be honoured and this through stable policy.

Rules in Keynes's schema really apply on two levels. There are the rules (conventions) by which we form our expectations and there are the rules which we must follow because of these conventions. Given that there is no objective basis for forming expectations people employ conventional assessments. The trick in Keynes's mind was to follow a sufficiently careful policy to ensure that the rules for forming expectations would yield the desired result. In this world of subjective expectations there was clearly no possibility of mechanical fine-tuning.

It remains to be seen, of course, whether this rhetoric of rules will find a place in the ongoing conversations about Keynes. The noisy dining hall of conversations will certainly never become rows of automatons reciting the same interpretation. But perhaps it is not too much to hope that several of the conversations might begin to converge as those concerned with different aspects of Keynes's thought begin to realize that they can profitably partake of each others' discussions. At first sight, the links between his theoretical and ethical thought is not a likely candidate for discussion, but it seems to help in understanding both areas more clearly.[10]

NOTES

1. The best example of the work considering Keynes's methodology is probably the collection of essays edited by T. Lawson and M. Pesaran (1985). See also Lawson (1985, 1987), Davis (1990) and Bateman (1990a).
2. This work includes Carabelli (1988), Fitzgibbon (1988), O'Donnell (1989a), Bateman (1988) and Davis (1990).
3. This section covers the same material as Bateman (1988).
4. O'Donnell (1989a, pp. 107–12) contains an interesting discussion of Keynes's attitude towards rules.
5. This section covers the same material as Bateman (1987). The story which the section tells of Keynes's self-proclaimed change of heart about the objective nature of probabilities has recently been challenged by O'Donnell (1989a, 1990), Carabelli (1988), Lawson (1985), and Hamouda and Smithin (1988a). Although every philosopher who has written on Keynes's work has accepted Keynes's proclamations at face value, it is worth considering these denials by economists given the centrality of the question to interpreting Keynes's work. I take the best of these denials to be O'Donnell (1990) and have critiqued this argument in Bateman (1990b).
6. Keynes's eventual acceptance of the importance of rules was in the spheres of both personal conduct and policy rules. Their importance in both spheres springs from his application of the model of mathematical expectations in both spheres; once he abandoned the idea of objective probabilities in either sphere, it becomes crucial to have social norms which direct people in making decisions in which the use of subjective probabilities could lead to undesirable outcomes.
7. The purpose of this paper is only to show the *analytical basis* for Keynes's change of heart regarding rules. It seems almost certain that Keynes's increasing concern with the necessity of rules came from experience in the political arena. This might have begun with his experience at Versailles, but one can certainly see the seeds for his concern with rules to control unstable investment in his experience with the Macmillan Committee. Peter Clarke (1989) tells the story very well of how Keynes became increasingly concerned with business confidence in the course of the Committee's work. Allan Meltzer (1989) traces Keynes's concern with rules to as early as 1923 in the *Tract*. Regardless of the source of this concern, the purpose of this paper is only to trace the analytical bases which allow Keynes to translate this concern to theory.
8. Helburn's essay in this volume traces Keynes's analytical concern with rules to very different sources.
9. It is also a major conclusion of Meltzer (1989) that *The General Theory* is largely concerned with establishing policy rules. The primary difference between the interpretation there and the one here is that Meltzer makes no effort to examine the analytical basis for this outcome in Keynes's own thinking on probability. Instead, he relies on the *canard* that Keynes always held a subjective theory of probability

and proceeds from this starting-point to attempt to show that Keynes's arguments are similar in nature to those of the rational expectationists.

10.   This is obviously the point of several of the essays in this volume and of the other work by the contributors.

5. Keynes's Weight of Argument and its Bearing on Rationality and Uncertainty

Rod O'Donnell[1]

On 30 October 1907, shortly before submitting his first fellowship dissertation, Keynes wrote to Lytton Strachey.

> I found yesterday that the new relation which you won't allow had also been thrown out as a suggestion by the great Meinong. So I have added an appendix of 4 pages about it.[2]

This appendix was Keynes's earliest treatment of his new concept, the weight of argument. It was some time, however, before the occasionally difficult infant received a lasting name. In the first dissertation (December 1907), it was called the 'intensity' of a probability, but in the second (December 1908) it was termed, rather confusingly, 'the value' of a probability. This was modified to 'evidential value' in an undated draft of the *Treatise on Probability* (hereafter *TP*), before becoming 'weight of argument', or 'weight', in the *TP* itself in 1921.[3] The latter remained Keynes's preferred terminology, although traces of the earlier appellations remain in his subsequent writings. This hesitancy over an appropriate name for his new concept is not without analytical significance. It reflects a certain lack of philosophical clarity about the concept – a lack at which Keynes himself hints and which, I think, is likely to emerge in the mind of anyone closely examining his discussion.[4] That he himself remained *somewhat* unclear is evident from his frank opening remark in the *TP*: 'The question to be raised in this chapter is somewhat novel; after much consideration I remain uncertain as to how much importance to attach to it' (*CW*, VIII, p. 77). And, in a sometimes misinterpreted remark, he also expressed doubt as to whether the theory of weight had 'much practical significance' *(CW,* VIII, p. 83). However, as will be shown below, the concept clearly *does* have importance in his writings, both in the *TP* and in the *General Theory* (hereafter *GT*). The overall impression Keynes conveys is one of a mixture of confidence and puzzlement – intuitively, the concept seems important and relevant, but when it comes to understanding it fully, it proves somewhat slippery.

The first part of this paper outlines the concept of weight and its basic properties. Here I shall argue that weight is one of the indefinables of Keynes's philosophical system, and be critical of interpretations which define it in terms of something else, such as a quantity of evidence. The second and third parts discuss the various ways in which weight bears on rationality and uncertainty, the second part concentrating on the *TP*, the third part on the *GT*. Here I shall argue that weight is linked to one of the several senses of uncertainty in Keynes's writings, and I shall criticize those writers who attempt to explain Keynes's uncertainty solely in terms of weight. I shall also criticize those interpretations which suggest that Keynes assumed agent irrationality in the *GT*, and contend that a better interpretation of Keynes comes from a broader approach in which different *forms* of rationality are recognized. To a significant, but not complete, extent these forms are dependent on the weight of argument.

While Keynes wrote a reasonable amount on weight, his reflections are far from voluminous. The main source documents are his two fellowship dissertations, draft chapters of the *TP*, the *TP* itself, the *GT*, and his 1938 correspondence with Townshend. None of these, however, contain lengthy commentaries. Chapter 6 in the *TP* is short (only eight and a half pages) and fairly condensed. Also noteworthy is the fact that the concept does not explicitly surface in any of his other unpublished philosophical writings, or in any of his published economic writings prior to the *GT*.

THE CONCEPT AND PROPERTIES OF WEIGHT

One of the central objects of the *TP* was the development of a general theory of logic dealing with rational but non-conclusive argument. Such arguments, according to Keynes, reposed on probabilities conceived as logical relations expressing the degree of support that the relevant data *h* of an argument gave to its conclusion *a*. On this view, probabilities are highly data-dependent. The same conclusion *a* may involve a number of probabilities, a/h_1, a/h_2, a/h_3, and so on, depending on the amount of information available to the individual. When new data favourably relevant to *a* are added to *h*, the probability of *a* relative to the new *h* will rise, but should additional information introduce evidence unfavourably relevant to *a,* the probability of *a* relative to the new *h* will decline.

Data thus occupy a central position in the logical theory of probability. This centrality encourages the idea that, in addition to their probabilities, non-conclusive arguments possess a second characteristic, one concerned not with the relation between *a* and *h,* but with the size of *h* in some sense. This characteristic, which Keynes eventually called the weight of argument, represented an independent dimension in which arguments might be classified and compared, and which had some bearing on rationality.

The concept of weight is not entirely straightforward, however, and has several subtleties. Keynes introduced it as follows:

> As the relevant evidence at our disposal increases, the magnitude of the probability of the argument may either decrease or increase, according as the new knowledge strengthens the unfavourable or the favourable evidence; but *something* seems to have increased in either case – we have a more substantial basis upon which to rest our conclusion. I express this by saying that an accession of new evidence increases the *weight* of an argument. New evidence will sometimes decrease the probability of an argument but it will always increase its 'weight' (*CW*, VIII, p. 77).

One point in this passage is immediately clear. Weight and probability are independent characteristics of an argument – as the amount of available information expands, weight will always increase, whereas probability may rise or fall. Weight reflects the total amount of information, but probability depends on the balance between its favourable and unfavourable parts. As Keynes metaphorically put it, weight measures 'the sum' of the favourable and unfavourable evidence whereas probability measures 'the difference' (*CW*, VIII, p. 84) .

However, beyond this point, the passage requires careful reading to avoid a misconception. It is tempting to slip into the notion that the weight of argument and the data *h* are identical, and that the term 'weight of evidence' can be used as a non-problematic substitute for 'weight of argument'. After all, as *h* rises, so also does weight. But from this necessary connection, it does not follow that the two can be equated. What Keynes actually says in the above passage is that as the data expands, *something* increases at the same time, this 'something' being the weight of argument. The word 'something', which Keynes himself italicized, does not signify *h* but some other concept, namely weight. Thus weight is not defined in terms of *h*. And when one searches the *TP* for a definition there is none to be found. The result is a concept, according to Keynes, which exists, which can be intuitively grasped, but which is left undefined as a 'something'. The inevitable conclusion is that the weight of argument is one of the fundamental indefinables (along with probability and goodness) of Keynes's philosophical system.

That weight and h are not synonymous terms is supported by further considerations. One is Keynes's symbolism, a matter about which he was quite particular since he believed that careful symbolism helped avoid errors of thinking. His symbol for the weight of argument is $V(a/h)$, the ' value ', to use the older expression, of the argument, a/h. Weight is not symbolized by h or by $V(h)$ as one might expect if weight were synonymous with, or defined in terms of, a quantity of evidence. A second consideration is provided by Keynes's rules for comparing the weights of arguments, a matter to be discussed below. One of these rules denies that the weights of arguments of the form a/h and ab/h can be compared, while another states that arguments of the form a/h and b/h do not always have the same weight. Neither of these rules makes sense if weight is the same as h, for then all of the above arguments would have the same weight. A way of clarifying these rules which avoids the error of conflating weight with h *is* provided below. It also deserves pointing out that while Keynes occasionally uses the term 'evidential weight', this is elliptical for evidential weight of argument and is not synonymous with 'evidence' or 'weight of evidence'.

The distinction between weight and evidence, and the indefinability of the former in Keynes's scheme, has been stressed because much of the philosophy of evidence requirement that refers to Keynes ignores them. Lakatos (1968a, p. 345), Levi (1973, p. 141) and Popper (1972, p. 406; 1983, p. 393n) all conflate weight of argument with weight of evidence and overlook its indefinability. It is important to point out the error because in dealing with philosophical topics economists often rightly follow the lead given by philosophers; it just so happens that on this point some philosophers have produced a mistaken interpretation.[5]

But while weight and relevant data are not identical, they are necessarily positively correlated. They are ' correlative terms', as Keynes puts it, for as the relevant h increases, weight necessarily moves in the same direction: '... to say that a new piece of evidence is "relevant" is the same thing as to say that it increases the "weight" of the argument' (*CW*, VIII, p. 78). In determining when evidence is relevant, Keynes advanced two criteria, a simple one and a 'stricter' one (*CW*, VIII, p. 59). On the simple criterion, h_1 is irrelevant to a if its addition leaves the probability unchanged ($a/hh_1 = a/h$); otherwise, if $a/hh_1 \neq a/h$, h_1 is relevant. This, however, can generate counterintuitive conclusions in various cases, one such occurring when h_1 can be decomposed into a favourably relevant part and a counterbalancing unfavourably relevant part. To overcome the difficulty, Keynes introduces a 'theoretically preferable' criterion which enables one to 'regard evidence as relevant, part of which is favourable and part unfavourable, even if, taken as a whole, it leaves the probability unchanged' (*CW*, VIII, p. 78).[6]

A second important property of weight as an attribute of an argument, as noted above, is that it is independent of probability: '... the weighing of the amount of evidence is quite a separate process from the balancing of the evidence for and against' (*CW*, VIII, p. 80). The effect of adding new relevant evidence to an argument is twofold – weight is always augmented, but probability may increase, decrease or remain the same depending on the effect of the evidence on the probability.[7]

The Measurement of Weight

Is the weight of argument susceptible of measurement and, if so, in what sense and under what conditions? Keynes replies that it is capable of measurement but that, just as with probability, the scope for measurement is highly restricted. Cardinal comparison is not mentioned at all, presumably because it seems impossible to discover a satisfactory method of reducing items of information of diverse kinds to a common numerical standard. Instead, Keynes's discussion focuses entirely on ordinal comparisons, where he finds that such comparisons are possible but only in the following two cases:

1. When the arguments are of the form a/h and a/hh_1. That is, the same conclusion and the evidence of one is a subset of that of the other. If the additional evidence h_1 is relevant, $V(a/hh_1) > V(a/h)$; but if h_1 is irrelevant, the two weights are equal.
2. When equiprobable alternatives are determined to exist by the principle of indifference. In these cases of numerical probabilities (arising in games of chance and the like), $a/h = b/h$ and $V(a/h) = V(b/h)$.

Beyond these two cases, however, Keynes does not think it possible to lay down any general rules. Thus, in the absence of further information, it is not possible to compare the weights of arguments of the following forms – those with different, overlapping conclusions and the same data (say a/h and ab/h); those with the same conclusion but where one evidence set does not entirely embrace the other (say a/h_1 and a/h_2); and arguments with different conclusions and different data (say c/h_3 and d/h_4). And even when $a/h = b/h$, Keynes takes care to point out that there is no general rule necessarily stipulating that $V(a/h) = V(b/h)$ (*CW*, VIII, pp. 79, 80). In Keynes's theory the measurement of weight is thus an even more problematic and restricted affair than the measurement of probability.

Considerable light is thrown on the concept of weight and its measurement, however, by another characteristic of weight that Keynes all too briefly mentions. This is the idea that weight is positively related to the nearness of an argument to either proof or disproof. The closer a/h *is* to either 1 (proof) or 0 (disproof), the higher its weight must be. Keynes gives two examples to illustrate the point. The first compares the weights of the arguments $ab/h = 0$ and $a/h > 0$. Here $V(ab/h) > V(a/h)$ on the grounds that ab/h *is* ' nearer' to one extremity (zero) of the probability scale than a/h which occupies an intermediate position. That is, regardless of the fact that h *is* the same, ab is disproved and is therefore closer to proof or disproof than a whose truth-value remains uncertain. The second example concerns propositions and their contradictories. In this case it is always true that $V(a/h) = V(-a/h)$, where $-a$ *is* the contradictory of a, since evidence which tends to prove a will tend, at the same time and to the same extent, to disprove $-a$, thus making the distance a is from proof equal to the distance $-a$ is from disproof.

The way in which this notion of nearness to proof or disproof helps illuminate Keynes's indefinable and its measurement may be explained as follows. Consider Keynes's two rules for the comparison of weights, the first of which states that $V(a/hh_1) > V(a/h)$. The reason why the former weight is the greater is not merely that hh_1 exceeds h, but that the probability a/hh_1, regardless of whether it has risen or fallen, is nearer to proof or disproof than the probability a/h. The addition of relevant evidence h_1 pushes the probability closer to either 1 or 0. In the case of Keynes's second rule, a/h and b/h are equally close to proof or disproof since a and b are equiprobable alternatives; throwing a six with a (presumed) fair dice is no more certain or impossible than throwing a 3.

It is also possible to explain in this way all the cases that Keynes excludes from rules of general comparison. The focus is again not on h, but on the nearness of the argument to either proof or disproof. Comparison of weights is not possible in the cases previously mentioned (a/h and ab/h; a/h_1 and a/h_2; c/h_3 and d/h_4) because there is no way of determining, in the absence of additional information, the relative proximities of these arguments to either proof or disproof. However, if we were given further information to the effect that in any one of these cases the two probabilities were equal, then we might be able to say that the weights of the two arguments were equal. For example, if $a/h = b/h$ then $V(a/h) = V(b/h)$. But even here one must tread carefully. Keynes takes care to point out that this only holds if $a/h = b/h$ follows from a single application of the principle of indifference. He gives a brief example to explain why weights could be different when two applications of the principle of indifference are involved (*CW*, VIII, p. 79), but his example is far from transparent.

Some Additional Properties of Weight

The weight of argument possesses other characteristics worthy of attention. It has, to begin with, a *minimum* (non-zero) limit constituted by the meaning of the proposition standing as conclusion, *a*. Meanings constitute a form of relevant knowledge in Keynes's epistemology and therefore enter the data *h*; it is upon such data alone that Keynes's *a priori* probabilities are based. The *maximum* possible limit of weight is not discussed in the *TP* but this would presumably occur when all evidence relevant to the conclusion is known. In a deterministic world it would, for example, obtain when *a* could be completely proved or disproved, that is, when probability equals 1 or 0.[8]

Nor does Keynes explicitly remark on the epistemological status of weight, although it can be inferred that, like his other indefinables such as probability and goodness, weight is an objective concept independent of individual opinion. The 'something' that constitutes weight exists in an external realm of philosophical concepts and does not reside solely in the subjective mind of the individual. And when comparison of weight is possible, there is only one true answer as to whether one weight is greater than, equal to, or less than the other; it is not a matter of opinion that can vary between individuals.

The relationship of weight to probable error, however, is one that Keynes does address. At a theoretical level, weight has no connection at all with probable error in his theory. Not only may a rise in weight be associated with either an increase or decrease in probable error, but the two concepts differ significantly as regards their numericalness. Consequently, determining probable error is 'intrinsically a different problem' from determining weight (*CW*, VIII, p. 81). But on a practical level, a 'casual' connection can arise in 'a limited class of cases'.

> The connection between probable error and weight, such as it is, is due to the fact that in scientific problems a large probable error is not uncommonly due to a great lack of evidence, and that as the available evidence increases there is a tendency for the probable error to diminish. *In these cases* the probable error may conceivably be a good practical measure of the weight (*CW*, VIII p. 81, emphasis added).

Examples are provided by sampling exercises, an increase in sample size increasing weight and diminishing probable error. Keynes does not discuss variance, but the relationship between weight and variance may be described in the same terms as that between weight and probable error – no conceptual connection, but possible practical association in certain situations.

Lastly, there is a characteristic of weight which is of particular importance in Keynes's later writings. This is the idea that weight of argument is related to the reliability of probabilities, and hence, by extension, to the amount of confidence we may place in them. When confronted with two arguments of the form a/h and a/hh_1, we are entitled to regard the latter as more reliably founded and as worthy of greater confidence because it is grounded on more information. In this sense, weight refers to the 'well-foundedness' of the probability. That is, irrespective of the magnitudes of the probabilities, higher weights generate more reliable arguments, or probabilities in which we may place higher degrees of confidence. It should be noted, however, that while Keynes refers to 'reliability' (in regard to Nitsche) in Chapter 6 and describes higher weight as providing 'a more substantial basis upon which to rest our conclusion' (*CW*, VIII, p. 77), he does not actually employ the word 'confidence'. Nevertheless, it seems a legitimate extension of his ideas in this context.[9]

WEIGHT-RELATED ASPECTS OF THE *TREATISE ON PROBABILITY*

As an independent characteristic of argument, weight would be expected to play some role in influencing rational belief and behaviour. This is indeed so, and three different situations may be distilled from the discussion in the *TP*.

The first is the case of the same conclusion a to which increasing amounts of evidence, $h_1, h_2, \ldots h_n$, are relevant, each successive evidence set exceeding but including the previous set. A typical example would be the accumulation of evidence over time in research investigating a particular hypothesis. Here Keynes proposes what I have previously called (1989a, p.74) *the principle of maximum weight*. On this principle, the rational course in decision-making is to use the probability with the greatest weight of argument.

> Bernoulli's second maxim, that we must take into account all the information we have, amounts to an injunction that we should be guided by the probability of that argument, amongst those of which we know the premises, of which the evidential weight is the greatest (*CW*, VIII, p. 83; also 345).

Thus in the above case, the rational agent will choose a/h_n, a choice consistent with the first rule for comparing weights. Keynes does not, however, give any reasons why the principle should be adopted, a lack noted by Broad (1922, p.78) who wished Keynes had discussed 'why we feel it rational to prefer an argument of greater weight to one of less of weight'. Keynes seemed to have regarded the principle as self-evidently true.[10]

The second link between weight and rationality derives from the first. If it is rational to base decisions on probabilities with maximum weight, should we then not maximize weight prior to forming probabilities? Ought we not devote our energies to collecting as much information beforehand instead of resting content with what is currently available? Locke apparently thought we should, but Keynes was of the view that no general rule could be laid down in this area.

> ... should not this [Bernoulli's second maxim] be re-enforced by a further maxim, that we ought to make the weight of our arguments as great as possible by getting all the information we can? It is difficult to see, however, to what point the strengthening of an argument's weight by increasing the evidence ought to be pushed. We may argue that, when our knowledge is slight but capable of increase, the course of action which will, relative to such knowledge, probably produce the greatest amount of good, will often consist in the acquisition of more knowledge. But there clearly comes a point when it is no longer worth while to spend trouble, before acting, in the acquisition of further information, and there is no evident principle by which to determine *how far* we ought to carry our maxim of strengthening the weight of our argument (*CW*, VIII, p. 83).[11]

Thus, on some occasions, the sensible course will be to collect more information and postpone decision-making, while on others it will be to proceed with decisions because further evidence collection is too costly. There being no general rule here, decisions are to be made according to circumstances, a stance consistent with the consequentialism developed later in the *TP*. Beyond such general considerations, however, Keynes offered no further analysis of what he admitted to be a 'very confusing problem'.

The third application of weight is in the theory of rational action. After entering a criticism of mathematical expectations, Keynes assigned weight a positive role in a more general theory of rational behaviour. The mathematical expectations doctrine was criticized as a general approach because, among other things, it ignored weight in the determination of desirable courses of action (*CW*, VIII, p. 344). What was needed, in Keynes's view, was a more general, but still consequentialist, theory which was directed towards the maximization of probable goodness and which was capable of taking some account, as occasion warranted, of two of the novel concepts of the *TP*, weight of argument and moral risk. The bearing of these two concepts on rational action was that both greater weight and lesser risk provided reasons for choosing one course over others.

> There seems ... a good deal to be said for the conclusion that, other things being equal, that course of action is preferable, which involves least risk and about the results of which we have the most complete knowledge.... A high weight and the absence of risk increase *pro tanto* the desirability of the action to which they refer (*CW*, VIII, pp. 347–8).

But Keynes acknowledged that specifying precisely how weight and moral risk were to be taken into account presented considerable problems. As regards weight, he noted:

> The question appears to me to be highly perplexing, and it is difficult to say much that is useful about it. But the degree of completeness of the information upon which a probability is based does seem to be relevant, as well as the actual magnitude of the probability, in making practical decisions (*CW*, VIII, p. 345).

It is often not realized that it is to *this* context that his earlier remarks, in Chapter 6 of the *TP* about not being sure that the theory of weight had much practical significance refer. This is evident from the relevant paragraph in Chapter 6 and its accompanying footnote (*CW*, VIII, p. 83 & n1). It is not that Keynes thought weight had little significance to practical situations in general, as Levi (1973, ch.9) implies, or that he thought it had no relevance to practical decision-making. Although his wording was imprecise, his real difficulty was in specifying *how* weight was to be taken into account in decision-making and of thinking of 'clear examples' of this. Nevertheless Keynes makes some suggestions. He certainly thinks that weight and risk ought to be considered 'in marginal cases', and he suggests that they might exert 'some influence in other cases also' (*CW*, VIII, pp. 347–8). By marginal cases it seems clear that he means situations in which two courses of action emerge with equal probable goodnesses. Here weight and risk are sometimes capable of combining straightforwardly to act as tie-breakers. When, for example, one of the equal courses is endowed with both greater weight and lesser risk, it is to be rationally preferred. However, weight and risk are independent of each other, and difficulties arise when their effects pull in opposite directions – say, when one course has higher weight but greater risk. Some principle for combining their respective influences is thus required for these marginal cases, and possibly also for non-marginal cases. But Keynes admits that the difficulty lies in the 'lack of any principle for the calculation of the degree of their influence'. He toys with a mathematical formula for a 'conventional coefficient', but knowing this to be unsatisfactory as a general approach, he makes his final appeal to a direct judgement of the situation as a whole (*CW*, VIII, pp. 348–9).[12]

The influence of weight and risk on rational decision-making throws additional light on Keynes's stances in all those areas involving a choice between 'the moral value of speculative and cautious action' (*CW*, VIII, p. 347). Here, weight and risk will often join forces to speak in favour of prudence. Suppose that cautious and speculative courses of action have equal probable goodnesses, say $p_1 A_1 = p_2 A_2$ respectively, where $p_1 > p_2$ and $A_1 < A_2$. In such cases, the cautious course has the lower moral risk, for moral risk equals $pA(1-p)$. And, for a variety of reasons, it will frequently happen that the amount of specific information supporting p_1 will be greater than that supporting p_2. There may, for example, be more experience relating to cautious action than to speculative, or the benefits of cautious action may be more definite and discernible in the short term compared to the vaguer and more distant benefits of some forms of the latter. In such cases, weight and risk will combine to tip the balance in favour of the cautious alternative. Apart from having applications to his economics, these ideas are also relevant to Keynes's politics, particularly his strong preference for gradual reform over violent revolution.[13]

Weight is also important in explicating the concept of uncertainty in Keynes's scheme. The *TP's* treatment of this all-pervasive theme is quite complex, however. I shall describe it as both multidimensional and multi-levelled. It is multidimensional in that, on any given level of analysis, there are two aspects of uncertainty. The first is linked to probability – being uncertain about the truth or falsity of a particular proposition, we fall back on its probability as indicating the degree of rational belief we may have in it. The second sense is related to weight or relevant evidence. Here our ignorance is represented by 'the degree of completeness of the information' (*CW*, VIII, p. 345) upon which our argument is based. It is evident in the partial absence of relevant knowledge – we possess some knowledge but we know it is typically incomplete, and we may also be unsure as to the extent of its incompleteness. Our uncertainty in this sense is reflected in the degree of confidence we place in the argument.[14]

Uncertainty is also *multilevelled* in the sense that it may inhabit different levels of analysis, of which again two principal ones may be isolated. The first I shall describe as the *determinate* level, a level ruled by strong rationality. The term 'probabilistic uncertainty' encapsulates part, but not all, of this concept. On this level, reason or intuitive judgement is able to achieve determinate answers to the tasks it is called upon to perform within Keynes's theory. It is capable, for example, of perceiving the necessary probability relations, so drawing these into the realm of known probabilities. Second, when required, it is able to compare the probabilities and weights of different arguments and, third, it is adequate to the tasks involved in ranking the probable goodnesses of wholes, such wholes including probability, goodness, weight and moral risk. It is on this level of determinacy and strong rationality that most of the analysis of the *TP* is conducted.

However, a second level of analysis is recognized in the *TP*, although it receives far less discussion and is often overlooked by commentators. This may be described as the *indeterminate* level, a level which is inhabited by forms of weak rationality, and of which a part is reflected in the term 'non-probabilistic uncertainty'. Here the strong form of reason is defeated, either by an insufficiency of mental power to perform the necessary intuitive judgements, or by the fact that such judgements are declared impossible by the relevant theory. For example, the rational individual may lack sufficient intellectual intuition to 'see' the probability relation, with the result that the probability remains invisible in the realm of unknown probabilities. This will typically happen when there is a paucity of relevant information (low weight) such that the individual cannot intuit the logical relation between this data and other propositions. Second, probabilities may belong to inherently non-comparable series, or no rules may be available for the comparison of weights. Third, in determining rational action, the individual may not be able to form non-numerical probable goodnesses on the whole, and to rank these ordinally. In all such situations the strong form of rationality is powerless. The rational agent now knows far less than before, and a qualitatively different, more wide-ranging, and more radical type of uncertainty comes into existence. Previously there were clear, if probabilistic, answers, but now there are no determinate answers at all. Ignorance has deepened and uncertainty has broadened its sway.

However, one should avoid the temptation of concluding that this necessarily forces individuals into irrationality. The mere fact that ignorance has increased does not, of itself, imply irrationality. Rational individuals adapt to their circumstances, and will thus adopt new forms of behaviour – forms which I have grouped under the heading of 'weak rationality'. This involves such modes of behaviour as the following of social customs, conventions, rules-of-thumb or apparently better-informed opinion, or of allowing more arbitrary procedures such as coin-tossing or pure caprice to decide. Under the circumstances, these responses are compatible with reason and are not irrational *per se*. In addition, rational individuals will be aware that such responses are based on imposed ignorance and have no strong foundations in either certain or probable knowledge and will therefore have a low, and easily shaken, degree of confidence in them. If some other type of behaviour seems more appropriate or temporarily more successful than that currently being followed, significant shifts in behaviour can readily occur. This, of course, is highly relevant to the long-term expectations of the *GT*.[15]

WEIGHT-RELATED ASPECTS OF THE *GENERAL THEORY*

It is striking that the concept of weight is not explicitly referred to in any of Keynes's published economic writings prior to the *GT*. It certainly has an implicit presence throughout this period (and subsequently), in that Keynes always sought to base his own reasoning on all the evidence available and criticized others for not so doing, and in that he constantly pushed practical measures to expand society's information base. The first of these reflects his 'principle of maximum weight', while the second represents the attempt to maximize relevant evidence in general so that the foundations of inference could be improved.[16] But, despite this implicit concern with weight, the concept is given little or no *analytical* role in his writings on economy theory.

The change comes with the *GT*. In the work in which he sought to break radically new theoretical ground, he deploys weight as an explanatory concept in economics for the first time. Its presence is unobtrusive, and its treatment far from transparent, but it nevertheless finally appears on-stage in a role reinforced by his subsequent correspondence with Townshend. Perhaps it was its unobtrusiveness in the *GT* together with the widespread ignorance of Keynes's philosophical work among economists (Townshend and Shackle excepted) that led to its neglect for so many years in the analysis of the *GT*. On the theoretical side of the *GT*, weight figures in three areas – uncertainty, confidence and liquidity preference.

As regards uncertainty, weight is important in providing analytical background to the concepts of long-term expectations and extreme or radical uncertainty. Keynes's first reference to weight is in relation to the meaning of extreme uncertainty (*CW*, VIII, p. 148 & n1), his stipulation being that 'very uncertain' is not to be translated as 'very improbable'. It must therefore have some other meaning and the reader is directed back to the *TP*'s chapter on weight. The implication is that 'very uncertain' refers to situations of very low weight of argument – that is, of great paucity or extreme incompleteness of relevant information. It is in this environment of extreme uncertainty as regards the distant future that long-term expectations are formed. This concept of extreme uncertainty, defined in terms of low weight, is clearly not precisely the same as the concept of irreducible uncertainty defined in the 1937 *QJE* article in terms of the non-availability of probabilities. But it is very easy to explain Keynes's dual usage and the manner in which the two concepts overlap if recourse is had to the doctrine of unknown probabilities of the *TP*. Logical probability relations can only be perceived, and therefore known, when sufficient information exists relative to the individual's mental ability. If mental ability cannot intuit the probability relation on the information available, the probability remains unknown. Such situations will typically occur when economic agents of given mental abilities inhabit informationally deprived environments. In situations of very low weight, or of hardly any relevant information, the ordinary individual will not be able to perceive the probability relation between a and h. Thus when weight is low, a/h will often be unknown. Of course, as made clear earlier, there is no logically necessary connection between low weight and unknown probabilities, but there is a strong practical connection. And that this is the appropriate link between these two notions of uncertainty is, I think, made clear in both the *GT* and the *QJE* summary. In the *GT*, Keynes speaks of the ' extreme precariousness of *the basis of knowledge* on which our estimates of prospective yield have to be made' and of the fact that *'our basis of knowledge* for estimating the yield ten years hence ... amounts to little and sometimes to nothing' (*CW*, VII, pp. 149–50, emphases added). The 'basis of knowledge' for estimating expectations here refers to *h* and hence to the weight of argument. The explicit connection to an absence of probabilities comes in 1937. The kind of uncertainty that Keynes emphasized was not to be equated with probabilistic uncertainty but with a more radical kind of uncertainty in which knowledge was so sparse that there was 'no scientific basis on which to form any calculable probability whatever. We simply do not know' (*CW*, XIV, pp. 113–4).[17]

However, extreme and irreducible uncertainty are not the only kinds deployed in the *GT*. Keynes also acknowledges other types of uncertainty – uncertainty when weight is high and uncertainty when probabilities are discernible. These types are particularly relevant to short-term expectations, those upon which the firm's 'daily' output and employment decisions depend. Such expectations are typically based on greater amounts of relevant information than their long-term counterparts, since 'a large part of the circumstances usually continue substantially unchanged from one day to the next' (*CW*, VII, p. 51). This represents uncertainty in a context of relatively high weight. It would also be quite possible for these short-term expectations to be based, as occasion permitted, on probabilities. Keynes's cryptic footnote in Chapter 3 suggests this (*CW*, VII, p. 24n3), as does a later remark in the context of liquidity (*CW*, VII, p. 240). And since Keynes often expressed the idea that expectations are based on induction (*CW*, VII, p. 148), it is perfectly possible for inductive projections to issue in probabilities under the right conditions. Thus those writers who relate the uncertainty in the *GT solely* to situations of low weight are mistaken.[18] Weight is certainly one factor, but, in the decision-making situations encompassed by the *GT*, weight can vary from low to high, and probabilities may be known or unknown. In pursuit of his general theory, Keynes wrote with all possible expectational situations in mind.

The same section in the *GT* that links low weight to extreme uncertainty also suggests that weight is linked to *confidence* in expectations. Long-term expectations are said to depend on two factors – on 'the most probable forecast', and on 'the *confidence* with which we make such forecasts' (*CW*, VII, p. 148). Even clearer authority for the confidence-weight connection is given in Chapter 17 where Keynes repeats the distinction between estimates of probabilities and our confidence in these estimates (*CW*, VII, p. 240 and n1). In the *GT*, the weight–confidence link takes the same form as that of the *TP* – namely, confidence and weight are directly related. The example Keynes gives is of a situation in which confidence is weak because, even though large changes are expected, we are 'very uncertain' (that is, there is low weight) regarding their precise form (*CW*, VII, p. 148); the missing information is thus *specific* information bearing on the exact nature of the anticipated changes. Although the discussion which introduces the weight–confidence link runs in terms of probability estimates and confidence, it is, I suggest, more consistent with Keynes's views taken as a whole to replace probabilities here with the more general concept of 'expectations', since expectations in Keynes's scheme (especially long-term expectations) can, and do, exist in the absence of probabilities. With this substitution the probability–weight dimensions of the *TP* may be aligned with the generalized expectation–confidence pair of the *GT*. In relation to the analysis of rationality developed above, it is with situations of low weight that weak rationality will most often be associated. Low weight implies weak confidence, and if it also generates irreducible or non-probabilified uncertainty, then rational individuals are forced into the strategies of weak rationality and the possibility of large shifts in behaviour.

In three successive years, during and after the *GT*, Keynes referred explicitly or implicitly to a connection between weight and liquidity preference. As this concept is fundamental to Keynes's critique of the classical dichotomy between real and monetary variables, the role of weight as an explanatory variable in the *GT* takes on additional significance. One would thus expect an examination of weight and its implications among those interpreters who stress liquidity preference as one of the most important characteristics of the *GT*. Yet the topic has been largely neglected until recently (Townshend and Shackle being early exceptions). The connection may be explained as follows. In his theory of interest rates, Keynes distinguished two premia which had to be paid to wealth-holders to induce them to part with their wealth – a risk premium and a liquidity premium. The difference between them was explained in terms of the probability–weight couple of the *TP*. Risk premium was associated with our 'best estimates of ... probabilities', whereas liquidity premium was linked to 'the confidence with which we can make them' (*CW*, VII, p. 240 and n1, also p. 226). The alignment was repeated again in 1938 when Keynes wrote to Townshend who had been attempting to come to grips with some of the relationships between the *GT* and *TP*.

> I am rather inclined to associate risk premium with probability strictly speaking, and liquidity premium with what in my *Treatise on Probability* I called 'weight'. An essential distinction is that a risk premium is expected to

be rewarded on the average by an increased return at the end of the period. A liquidity premium, on the other hand, is not even expected to be rewarded. It is a payment, not for the expectation of increased tangible income at the end of the period, but for an increased sense of comfort and confidence at the end of the period (*CW*, XXIX, pp. 293–4).

Providing a full analysis of how weight and liquidity preference are related is complex and would take us too far afield. But the basic idea may be briefly indicated. Since liquidity is the ease of disposal of an asset, liquidity premium is the amount asset-holders are willing to pay for this characteristic of the asset in order to obtain 'potential convenience or security' (*CW*, VII, p. 226). Now, liquidity will vary between assets, and its importance to asset-holders will vary with circumstances. When times are uncertain, in the sense that there is little specific information bearing on future changes, then weight will be low. Under these conditions, liquidity will be important to wealth-holders and there will be a movement to more liquid assets of which money is the most liquid. Weight and liquidity preference are thus inversely related. Low weight implies low confidence about future estimates and this enhances the appeal of liquidity. As Keynes put it in 1937:

> ... our desire to hold money as a store of wealth is a barometer of *the degree of our distrust* of our own calculations and conventions concerning the future....The possession of actual money lulls our disquietude; and the premium which we require to make us part with money is the measure of the degree of our disquietude (*CW*, XIV, p. 116, emphasis added).

Thus in situations of low weight, the liquidity premium of money rises and interest rates move upwards.

It follows that the level of investment is influenced by two weight-related variables whose effects work in the same direction. Through its link with confidence, weight affects the marginal efficiency of capital while, through its link to liquidity preference, it affects the rate of interest. The combined effect is analogous to the distance between two pincer jaws. Low weight reduces the marginal efficiency of capital and raises the rate of interest, thus squeezing investment from both sides (*CW*, VII, p. 316; XIV, p. 118). High weight, by contrast, widens the jaws and encourages investment by raising the marginal efficiency and lowering interest rates. Thus, given the importance of investment in the *GT*, the significance of weight is further reinforced. However, in discussing weight in the *GT*, it is worth remembering Keynes's remark, made in the context of confidence.

> There is ... not much to be said about the state of confidence *a priori*. Our conclusions must mainly depend upon the actual observation of markets and business psychology. This is the reason why the ensuing digression is on *a different level of abstraction* from most of this book. (*CW*, VII, p. 149, emphasis added)

That is to say, while confidence is vitally important, its further investigation requires a different level of analysis. Precisely how variations in weight actually influence market behaviour under various conditions is not so much a matter of *a priori* generalization as of empirical observation.

CONCLUSION

Despite his own asides, its relatively subordinate position in the *TP*, and its apparently minor role in the *GT*, Keynes's concept of the weight of argument is actually quite an important element in the architecture of his thought as a whole. It plays significant analytical roles in his theories of uncertainty and rationality, and it provides important underpinnings to his theories of investment and liquidity preference. but the concept requires careful analysis, for it is far from being totally translucent in either its philosophical or economic arenas. And, while recognizing its explanatory relevance to Keynes's theories, one should not inflate the concept with more significance than it actually possesses; it is not, for example, the whole foundation to Keynes's approach to uncertainty, although it is certainly an essential part of it.

NOTES

1.   I would like to thank King's College, Cambridge for permission to quote from the Keynes Papers, and the Australian Research Council for assistance with funding.
      While partly based on O'Donnell (1982) (which contained the first extensive analysis of weight and its links with Keynes's economics) and O'Donnell (1989a, chs 4, 6 and 12), the following discussion improves in one or two areas on the exposition of these earlier works. Readers are also referred to Carabelli (1988) which provides a discussion of weight; I shall indicate some of my points of disagreement with Carabelli's account in what follows. All references to Keynes's published writings are to the 29 volumes of the *Collected Writings of John Maynard Keynes* (1973–89) annotated as *CW*.

2.   Keynes Papers, King's College Library. Regarding historical priority for the introduction of the concept of weight or its equivalent, honours appear to belong

to C.S. Peirce in 1878 (1965, II, p. 421). Peirce, with whose writings on this particular topic Keynes appeared unacquainted, thus preceded Meinong and Nitsche to whose work in the 1890s Keynes attributed priority (*CW*, VIII, pp. 84–5). Following the publication of the *TP*, C.D. Broad penned a reminder to Keynes concerning his own contribution of 1914.

You will find that in ... my *Perception, Physics and Reality, I* did discuss what is substantially your distinction between Weight and Probability, and discussed it in in connexion with causal laws. I remember being horribly puzzled by it, and am quite sure that I said nothing of the least value. But, as you are interested in the history of the subject, I thought I would just mention this. (24 October 1921)

Keynes replied on 31 January 1922:

But I have of course read pretty carefully your "Perception, Physics and Reality," and I ought to have remembered it in my account of *Weight*. My excuse is that I wrote that chapter of my book a good many years ago and have not revised it, except verbally, in recent years. (Keynes Papers)

Keynes, of course, first developed his concept in 1907, preceding Broad in conception, if not publication.

3. For Keynes's early fellowship dissertation treatments of weight, see O'Donnell (1982, App. G; 1989, pp. 76–7), and Carabelli (1988, pp. 56–7, 261).

4. Broad was 'horribly puzzled' by the idea (see above footnote); to Hilpinen (1970, p. 118) the concept seemed possibly ambiguous; while Cohen (1985) has presented 12 questions (and answers) about his particular interpretation of Keynes's weight.

5. Care needs to be taken in approaching the modern literature on weight. First, the terms 'weight' and 'evidential value' now refer to a rather confusing variety of concepts, many of which bear little or no relation to Keynes's original idea. For example, Harrod (1974, p. 28) treats 'evidential value' and 'probability' as referring to the same relation. Good's several publications (e.g. 1950, ch. 6) define weight of evidence mathematically as a logarithm of a ratio of likelihoods. Cohen (1977) takes weight to be measured by inductive probabilities, while his 1985 work interprets weight as a degree of inferability from a conditional to an unconditional probability. All of these concepts are well removed from Keynes's. By ignoring these differences, Carabelli (1988, p. 260, n. 28) creates a misleading impression. Second, in those accounts which do discuss Keynes's concept, considerable confusion is sometimes evident; examples here include Ayer (1957) and Weintraub (1975, pp. 531–2).

6. For further discussion see O'Donnell (1989b), which also advances a means of rescuing Keynes's criteria from Popper's 'paradox of ideal evidence'. Carabelli's suggestion (1988, p. 56) that Keynes 'appeared actually to go so far as to redefine the concept of relevance ... in terms of weight' is, I believe, mistaken. Keynes's definitions of irrelevance and relevance are quite independent of the notion of weight and survive the latter's absence. From the fact that Keynes required weight and relevant evidence to be correlative, it does not follow that relevance is redefined in terms of weight.

7. For reasons discussed in O'Donnell (1989b), weight of argument may also increase even though probability (and hence nearness to proof or disproof) remains unchanged.

8. Maximum possible weight, however, is mentioned in Keynes (1907, p. 131): 'The maximum intensity [weight] is found when the probability is 1 or 0'.

9. The notion of reliability also figures in Keynes (1907, p. 130) where it is presented
    in different terms as a function of both probability and weight (intensity). For
    further discussion of the properties of weight, see O'Donnell (1989a, ch.4, and
    1989b). Carabelli's account (1988, p. 58) of that passage of the *TP* where Keynes
    speaks of individuals placing 'an excessive confidence' in certain kinds of con-
    clusions is based on a misinterpretation. Carabelli automatically connects the word
    'confidence' to weight, whereas the context (pp. 273–5) indicates that the word is
    here used in relation to probability or degrees of certainty. For example:

    'While we depreciate the former probability of beliefs which we no longer hold, we
    tend, I think, to exaggerate the present degree of certainty of what we still believe.
    … In the same way we, perhaps, put an excessive confidence in those conclusions
    – the existence of other people, … the law of gravity, or to-morrow's sunrise – of
    which, in comparison with many other beliefs, we are very well assured. We may
    sometimes confuse … practical certainty … with the … objective certainty of
    logic' (*CW*, VIII, p. 275).

    The relatively high probabilities of which Keynes is speaking here may, of course,
    be accompanied by high weight, but it is not necessary. Weight forms no part of his
    explanation in this and the surrounding passages.
10. When, however, the principle of maximum weight led to unknown probabilities,
    Keynes was prepared on practical grounds to admit 'an exception' to the principle
    so that known probabilities could be attained: 'When the relation of the conclusion
    to the whole of our evidence cannot be known, then we must be guided by its
    relation to some part of the evidence' (*CW*, VIII, p. 138), this part issuing in a
    known probability .
11. See also 'My Early Beliefs' (*CW*, X, p. 439).
12. For further discussion of these issues, including Keynes's conventional coefficient
    and his sometimes misunderstood attitude to mathematical expectations, see
    O'Donnell (1989a, pp. 106–33, 174, 263–5, 362).
13. For further discussion, see O'Donnell (1989a, chs. 13, 14).
14. In addition, we may be unsure of whether we ought to collect more information
    before proceeding to probability formation and decisions.
15. For further discussion of the distinction between strong and weak forms of
    rationality in both the *TP* and *GT*, see O'Donnell (1982; 1989a, chs. 4, 6, 12; and
    1989c).
16. For a discussion of the policy aspects of Keynes's notion of weight, see O'Donnell
    (1989b).
17. For a discussion of Keynes's concept of unknown probabilities, and their role in
    explicating irreducible uncertainty, see O'Donnell (1982; 1989a, chs. 3, 12; and
    1989c).
18. See, for example, Stohs (1980, pp.378, 381) and Brady (1987, pp. 43, 45).

6. Keynes's View of Economics as a Moral Science[1]

J.B. Davis

J.M. Keynes's theoretical understanding of economic method is one of the less well understood dimensions of his thought, both because Keynes's thinking, unlike that of most economists, was motivated by serious reflection on philosophical questions, and because Keynes's particular philosophical heritage – rooted as it was in early reflections on the philosopher G.E. Moore's *Principia Ethica* (Skidelsky, 1983) – was quite different from that of other Cambridge economists. Accordingly, although Keynes repeated the Cambridge view that economics is 'essentially a moral science and not a natural science' (*CW*, XIV, p. 297), that his own understanding of this notion and the method of economics had its origins in Keynes's own distinctive philosophical development perhaps suggests that Keynes transformed the Cambridge understanding of economic method, much as he transformed its conception of the economy.

Indeed, the methodological thinking of the Cambridge school did undergo considerable change in the space of three generations. At the end of the nineteenth century, Henry Sidgwick, Alfred Marshall, and John Neville Keynes, while hesitant to say economics sought universal laws on the model of natural science, nonetheless agreed that the empirical generalization of well established facts was a meaningful enterprise. Moreover, while each was aware of the role of value judgements in economics, there were few doubts concerning the validity of the normative–positive distinction, since Nassau Senior had come to underlie the idea of economics as an objective intellectual enterprise (Hutchison, 1981, pp. 46–62). By contrast, by the mid-twentieth century, it could well be said that many at Cambridge, in the words of Joan Robinson, believed that 'the positive and normative [could not] be sharply divided' (Robinson, 1962, p. 74), and that empirical work in economics was fraught with such difficulty that it could hardly be granted the role hoped for it at the beginning of the century. John Maynard Keynes, then, in virtue of his ties to both the earlier and later Cambridge economists, might naturally be thought the pivotal figure in this development.

Yet that Keynes's early philosophical thinking was largely formed under the impact of a reading of Moore's *Principia*, rather than in a conscientious study of the methodological convictions of the first generation of Cambridge economists, also suggests that Keynes's impact on the development of Cambridge methodological thinking may well have been relatively slight, given the fact that most economists at Cambridge after Keynes were either unacquainted with Moore's thought or simply uninterested in it. From this perspective, it might well be surmised that Keynes's considerable prestige, combined with his often severe criticism of his predecessors, discouraged interest in earlier methodological views, while, because Keynes's own early intellectual development was highly specific to a relatively private early philosophical experience, those attracted to Keynes's economic theories found it difficult to understand, or indeed feel much sympathy toward, those philosophical notions that ultimately came to underlie his view of economics as a moral science. In effect, later Cambridge economists had to innovate methodologically on a rather narrow doctrinal base, portions of which were likely to be altogether unappealing; and this, it could be concluded, makes a case for methodological discontinuity rather than development in the thinking about economics in the Cambridge school.

Moore, it is interesting to note, was a student of Sidgwick's in ethics at the turn of the century, and thus might have reinforced the Sidgwick–Marshall–Neville Keynes tradition in methodological thinking for J.M. Keynes. However, Sidgwick, whose seven-edition *The Methods of Ethics* was meant to synthesize the competing nineteenth-century moral philosophy traditions of J.S. Mill's utilitarianism and William Whewell's intuitionism (much as Marshall's authoritative *Principles* was meant to do for economics), never persuaded Moore that utilitarianism was coherent. As a result, Moore was to go on to revive the longstanding Cambridge Platonist tradition in his intuitionist *Principia*, and this set of ideas accordingly became the basis for Keynes's own early philosophical views. Indeed, Keynes's first major work, his *Treatise on Probability*, acknowledged (*CW*, VII, p. 20) and drew heavily on these Moorean beginnings (see O'Donnell, 1989a). In effect, then, Keynes's early philosophical thinking reached back in time over the first generation of Cambridge economists to a prior intellectual tradition at Cambridge. While this is arguably the reason Keynes's thinking about economic method has rarely been well explained, at the same time such beginnings provide new opportunities and resources for explaining Keynes's methodological thinking. What, then, were Keynes's early philosophical positions as they might relate to Keynes's later understanding of economic method?

KEYNES AND INDIVIDUAL JUDGEMENT

Keynes's 1938 characterization of economics as a moral science depends centrally upon conceiving economics as an art. In believing economics as art, however, one gives up the customary, natural science view of scientific method whereby one assumes individual instances are assimilated under general principles in relatively unproblematic fashion, and in its place rests greater emphasis upon the economist's capacity to exercise individual judgement regarding the novelty of the particular instance and the significance of data generally. Keynes suggests this in his 1938 statement in asserting that economics is 'a branch of logic, a way of thinking' (*CW*, XIV, p. 297), and by emphasizing his conception of what was involved in working with models of economic relationships. On this view, 'it is the essence of a model that one does *not* fill in real values for the variable functions' since to do this was to deprive a model of 'its generality and its value as a mode of thought' (Ibid.). Thus, an economic model for Keynes possesses an important element of indeterminacy which demands a capacity for individual judgement.

These convictions recall Keynes's earlier interest in individual judgement in his first reflections upon Moore's *Principia*. In his unpublished 1904 'Ethics in Relation to Conduct' paper, Keynes noted that Moore's recommendation to follow general commonsense rules of conduct when estimating the probable remote future effects of one's actions was often of little value when past experience bore little relation to the future. Indeed, Keynes went on to argue, probability statements ought not to be understood as simply registering what has occurred in some given proportion of past cases – in effect, the frequency theory of probability – but rather should be thought to represent one's estimate of the justification needed to make some statement, given the evidence at one's disposal. This implies that, even when one possesses some record of past experience regarding the likelihood of a future event, that evidence must nonetheless still be evaluated for its bearing on the conclusion at hand. Individual judgement accordingly took on particular significance for

Keynes from the outset of his intellectual career, so that, unlike others in the early Cambridge methodological tradition, Keynes always evidenced a considerable scepticism toward the use of *a posteriori* general principles in economics.

Keynes, however, was by no means of the opinion that legitimate general principles were non-existent. When, after some delay, he finally published his first and only philosophical study, the *Treatise on Probability*, Keynes asserted that probability relationships concerned '*a logical relation between two sets of propositions*' (*CW*, VII, p. 9), and that 'logic investigates the general principles of valid thought' (*CW*, VII, p. 3). What Keynes principally inherited from Moore, in fact, was the view that one could intuit, or grasp, in an act of individual judgement, general *a priori* relationships. This had been the central doctrine of *Principia Ethica*, where Moore had advanced the view that the good was *sui generis* and could only be grasped in and of itself. It was also the key position in Keynes's *Treatise*, where Keynes asserted that it was not possible to define probability, and that our knowledge of probability relationships depends upon our 'direct acquaintance' with logical relations between propositions (*CW*, VII, p. 13).

At the same time, in Keynes's mind this 'direct acquaintance' with the logical relationships between propositions retained an important connection with individual judgement. In arguing that probability relationships were objective and logical, Keynes had asserted that propositions were not probable in and of themselves, but rather only probable in relation to a particular body of knowledge embodied in other propositions. This implied, he noted, that probability theory possesses both subjective and objective dimensions, since

> …[W]hat particular propositions we select as the premises of *our* argument naturally depends on subjective factors peculiar to ourselves, [while] the relations, in which other propositions stand to these, and which entitle us to probable beliefs, are objective and logical (*CW*, VII, p. 4).

One's 'direct acquaintance' with the logical relations between propositions, then, depends importantly upon one's judgement concerning the evidence relevant to the desired probability judgement, since were our 'premisses' to change, we would generally discover ourselves directly acquainted with altogether different probability relationships. Keynes, in fact, took this to be a particular strength of his account.

Reflection will show that this account harmonises with familiar experience. There is nothing novel in the supposition that the probability of a theory turns upon the evidence by which it is supported; and it is common to assert that an opinion was probable on the evidence first at hand, but on further information was untenable. As our knowledge or our hypothesis changes, our conclusions have new probabilities, not in themselves, but relatively to these new premises (*CW*, VII, p. 8).

Thus, although the knowledge of probability relationships is a knowledge of general *a priori* logical principles, for Keynes this knowledge depends significantly upon the exercise of individual judgement.

All of this, Keynes went on to allow, imposes a certain relativity on probable knowledge that many might well surmise undermines the objective character of that knowledge.

Some part of knowledge – knowledge of our own existence or of our own sensations – is clearly relative to individual experience. We cannot speak of knowledge absolutely – only of the knowledge of a particular person. Other parts of knowledge – knowledge of the axioms of logic, for example – may seem more objective. But we must admit, I think, that this too is relative to the constitution of the human mind, and that the constitution of the human mind may vary in some degree from man to man. What is self-evident to me and what I really know, may be only a probable belief to you, or may form no part of your rational beliefs at all. And this may be true not only of such things as *my* existence, but of some logical axioms also. Some men – indeed it is obviously the case – may have a greater power of logical intuition than others (*CW*, VII, p. 14).

Keynes himself, of course, had little doubt that probability relationships were indeed objective. Yet whether this is the case, or whether Keynes was justified in thinking probability relationships objective, is not at issue here. Rather what is important to establish in the present context is whether there is a connection between this early emphasis Keynes places on individual judgement and what Keynes later understands about the need for individual judgement in economic models.

Certainly there is some question regarding whether or not Keynes's early philosophical thinking in this regard underlies his later thinking about economic method. In a later memoir, 'My Early Beliefs', Keynes repudiated some of his earliest philosophical thinking, especially in regard to his early expressions of confidence concerning the unimportance of relying on rules in judging what was right or wrong to do (*CW*, X, p. 446). Yet, although this might well seem to imply that less emphasis should be placed on the role of individual judgement in Keynes's later methodological thinking, or that individual judgement has an altogether different meaning for Keynes in his later work, the fact that in the same year (1938) as his 'My Early Beliefs' memoir Keynes also emphasized the importance of economists' capacity for individual judgement in his moral science characterization of economics suggests that his 'My Early Beliefs' critique was only concerned with the need to reassess the role of individual judgement in ethics proper. What is there then in what Keynes believes, distinctive of economics as a moral science that might be explained by Keynes's earlier philosophical ideas?

KEYNES ON INTROSPECTION AND JUDGEMENTS OF VALUE

In his 1938 characterization of economics as a moral science Keynes had also noted that economists make important use of introspection and judgements of value in their elaboration of economic models.

> I also want to emphasise strongly the point about economics being a moral science. I mentioned before that it deals with introspection and with values. I might have added that it deals with motives, expectations, psychological uncertainties. One has to be constantly on guard against treating the material as constant and homogeneous (*CW*, XIV, p. 300).

Economics is a moral science, then, because it is principally concerned with individuals' 'motives, expectations, [and] psychological uncertainties'. This explains why its subject matter is neither 'constant' nor 'homogeneous' and why the methods of natural science are inappropriate in economics. In effect, individuals' observed behaviour correlates in varying degree with their inner thoughts and intentions, so that economists must make significant use of introspection and judgements of value to be able to model individuals' behaviour. Introspection would enable the economist to ascribe motives to individuals, given their observed behaviour; and judgements of value would enable the economist to weigh the strength of individuals' commitments to various courses of action they have undertaken. Indeed, by consulting one's own case the economist could be expected to be able to 'segregate the semi-permanent or relatively constant factors from those which are transitory or fluctuating' (*CW*, XIV, pp. 296–7), since one would presumably have a clearer sense of an individual's motives by examining one's own likely motives in similar circumstances than by examining that individual's observed behaviour.

This perspective on economic method, as is well known, was not original to Keynes. The earlier Cambridge tradition of Sidgwick, Marshall and Neville Keynes had also emphasized introspection and judgements of value in economic method, although not much attention was devoted to examining the assumptions inherent in so doing.[2] Maynard Keynes, however, had good reason to think more carefully about the presuppositions of employing these methods, since introspection and judgements of value necessarily involve the exercise of individual judgement. That is, were one to assess another's motives by comparison with one's own case, this would clearly involve consulting one's own particular reaction to the particular circumstances encountered by another. Although reasoning by analogy in this manner certainly presupposes some knowledge of general relationships between individuals and their circumstances, the idea of case-by-case comparisons is nonetheless one that fundamentally concerns individual judgement.

Of course, there is much that is obscure in the idea of describing another's thoughts and intentions on the basis of one's own, and consequently whether it makes sense to say one can consult one's own case in order to evaluate that of others is not easily answered. On the one hand, if we are entirely unique and distinct individuals, then our individual circumstances will not be comparable.[3] On the other hand, if we do not differ significantly in our personal motives and valuations, then our behaviour should be sufficiently similar and transparent that it could well be treated as 'constant and homogeneous'. Keynes, of course, rejected this latter alternative. Indeed, his resistance to a natural science conception of economics stemmed precisely from his conviction that individuals were insufficiently similar in experience and circumstance for their thoughts and intentions to be predicted solely on the basis of their observable behaviour. How, then, was he able to argue that individuals were unique and distinct, and that at the same time introspective individual judgement was meaningful? Here, attention to Keynes's early philosophical thinking is again valuable.

Shortly after his first critique of Moore's *Principia Ethica* in his 1904 'Ethics in Relation to Conduct', Keynes completed two additional papers on the *Principia* for presentation to the Apostles, 'Miscellanea Ethica', dated July–September 1905 and 'A Theory of Beauty', dated September–October 1905. Although the papers investigate a number of difficulties in Moore's reasoning, for our purposes here, Keynes's conclusions regarding the proper application of Moore's principle of organic unities is of particular interest. Moore's principle of organic unities concerned the philosophical relationship between the value of a whole and the value of its parts, and stated that the value of 'a whole bears no regular proportion to the sum of the values of its parts' (Moore, 1903, p. 27). On the basis of this, Moore had gone on to argue that the universe as a whole constitutes an organic unity, and that it was accordingly one's moral duty to promote the good of the universe itself. Keynes found this conclusion unrealistic on the grounds that it made nonsense of the idea of moral duty. He then reasoned that the universe is not the organic whole whose value is at issue in ethics, and that this indicated that, where value is concerned, the principle of organic unities is only properly applied to the individual mind.

> In ethical calculation each individual's momentary state of mind is our sole unit. In so far as a state of mind has parts, to this extent I admit the principle of organic unities: it is the excellence of the state as a whole with which we are concerned. But beyond each individual the organic principle cannot reach.[4]

That is, the individual mind alone can be said to constitute an organic unity and, accordingly, moral duty only concerned promoting good states of mind in individuals.

The implications of Keynes's position, however, go beyond questions of ethics. That the individual mind is an organic unity implies both that its activity can only be explained in terms of principles appropriate to it as a whole and that the mind's parts – an individual's thoughts and feelings – are themselves principally to be explained in terms of the activity of the individual mind as a whole. Moreover, that for Keynes every individual mind constitutes an organic unity in and of itself, and that organic connection does not apply across individual minds implies that the principles that govern relationships between individual minds are different in nature from those appropriate to the individual mind. In effect, then, Keynes's redirection and reapplication of Moore's principles of organic unities effectively establishes a principle of autonomy for the individual as well as the foundations for an account of the nature of relationships between individuals. Individuals are distinct by virtue of the personal integrity of their mental experience, although, in a manner still to be explained, they share this autonomy with one another.

More formally, Keynes's redirection of Moore's organic unities principle provided Keynes with rudimentary criteria for individuating the individual economic agent via the determination of the conditions for individual identity through change. Generally speaking, one can claim one has successfully distinguished an individual of any sort when one can trace a set of characteristics that identify that individual through a period of change in other characteristics of that individual. Keynes's ascription of an organic unity to the mental contents of an individual accomplishes this since, though an individual's particular thoughts and feelings certainly change, for Keynes, because the individual mind always constitutes an organic unity and an individual's thoughts identify that individual, this implies that an individual's new thoughts and feelings remain the thoughts and feelings of that same individual.

This is of no little import. Although individuals are conventionally taken to be different and distinct from one another (often by virtue of their physical distinctiveness), whether one can in fact justify this distinctiveness is crucial to any methodological strategy that depends upon assessing the thinking and motives of others. Indeed, possessing criteria for individual identity is indispensable to any coherent explanation of introspection and judgements of value, since these methods presuppose some degree of intellectual autonomy on the part of the individual having recourse to them, in order to justify the claim that individuals can treat their own cases as a source of independent information regarding the motives and intentions underlying the observed behaviour of others. Put simply, the elaboration of individual identity criteria is a necessary, though not sufficient, condition for employing the methods of introspection and judgements of value. Such criteria are not sufficient in themselves, however, because establishing the distinctiveness of an individual's thought process does not also establish the representativeness of that thought process. That is, introspection and judgements of value can only be said to be authoritative if the thinking of the individual making such judgements can be said to be both distinct from and representative of the thinking of those individuals in economic life whose behaviour is to be explained. Does Keynes, then, also have a conception of the representative individual that would permit the economist taking his or her imagined responses to a set of circumstances confronted by others as typical of those individuals' likely responses to those circumstances?

KEYNES AND 'THE APPROXIMATE UNIFORMITY OF HUMAN ORGANS'

From quite early in his intellectual career Keynes did indeed struggle to define a sense in which an individual's thinking could be said to be typical of the thinking of individuals generally. Although, arguably, Keynes felt some difficulty in establishing this latter dimension of human thought (see Davis, 1991), nonetheless he clearly believed that an individual's thinking could be explained both in terms of a capacity for individual judgement reflecting upon that individual's own particular experience and a capacity to reason in a manner that might be said objective in an intersubjective sense. This is apparent in Keynes's 1905 'Miscellanea Ethica' paper, where Keynes draws a distinction between what an individual can think and feel and what an individual ought to think and feel.

> [I]t is plain that the idea and the emotion appropriate to any given sensation are partly dependent on the nature and past history of the individual who feels. This is obvious enough; we ought not all to have precisely similar states in similar physical circumstances; common sense and the commandments are agreed on that. But we can in many cases abstract that element which ought to vary from man to man. Assuming the approximate uniformity of human organs, we can often – say what, apart from peculiar circumstances, a man *ought* to think and feel: – not indeed what he *can* think and feel – that will *always* depend upon his nature and his past.

Thus Keynes allows a role for individual judgement, but also supposes that one can often say what another individual would likely think and feel, on the grounds that there exists an 'approximate uniformity of human organs'. Since individuals possess essentially the same constitution, it is not unreasonable to say that we often anticipate what another will think and do under normal circumstances, although this does not of course preclude unexpected behaviour on the part of individuals, since an individual's behaviour is also to be explained by his or her 'nature and past history'. But economics surely is concerned with explaining average behaviour and thus, on Keynes's view, the economist would not be unjustified in supposing introspection and judgements of value produce defensible opinions about agents' motives and intentions.

This notion of a common intellectual and motivational constitution, it should be noted, has already been seen to underlie Keynes's thinking in his *Treatise on Probability*. There Keynes asserts that 'logic investigates the general principles of valid thought' which form the basis for rational belief. While probability judgements do possess a subjective dimension in the individual's selection of premises, this should not obscure the objective character of probability in Keynes's view.

> But in the sense important to logic, probability is not subjective. It is not, that is to say, subject to human caprice. A proposition is not probable because we think it so. When once the facts are given which determine our knowledge, what is probable or improbable in the circumstances has been fixed objectively, and is independent of our opinion. The theory of probability is logical, therefore, because it is concerned with the degree of belief which it is *rational* to entertain in given conditions, and not merely with the actual beliefs of particular individuals, which may or may not be rational (*CW*, VIII, p. 4).

Keynes's position in this regard, it is true, is not invulnerable to the considerable emphasis Keynes also placed on individual judgement in the *Treatise*, especially in his above noted discussion of 'the relativity of knowledge to the individual' (VIII, p. 18). Yet at the same time, Keynes obviously saw two dimensions to an individual's thinking – subjective and objective sides – and this conviction is what is at issue in an analysis of his claims for economics as a moral science.

Indeed, when Keynes came to confront F.P. Ramsey's criticism of the *Treatise on Probability* as indefensibly objectivist, Keynes allowed that there was something to Ramsey's complaint, while still insisting that Ramsey's account of probabilities as subjective was nonetheless lacking in an important regard.

> Ramsey argues, as against the view which I put forward, that probability is concerned not with objective relations between propositions but (in some sense) with degrees of belief, and he succeeds in showing that the calculus of probabilities simply amounts to a set of rules for ensuring that the system of degrees of belief which we hold shall be a consistent system. Thus the calculus of probabilities belongs to formal logic. But the basis of our degrees of belief – or the *a priori* probabilities, as they used to be called – is part of our human outfit, perhaps given to us merely by natural selection, analogous to our perceptions and our memories rather than to formal logic (*CW*, X, pp. 338–9).

Thus, although it may not be possible to speak of objective probability relations between propositions in the manner desired in the *Treatise*, for Keynes even Ramsey's view should not be regarded as a fully subjective one, since it still presupposes 'our human outfit' is somehow responsible for the rules that define the calculus of probabilities. How 'our human outfit' might function to produce a coherent, intersubjective calculus of probabilities, admittedly, is not explained by Keynes. It is clear, nonetheless, that despite the considerable weight Keynes placed on individual judgement in his philosophical thinking, this somehow always operated against a backdrop of intersubjective intellectual capacity among individuals.

This emphasis should be placed in proper perspective. When Keynes argued in 1938 that economics is a moral science, he specifically contrasted his view to that of Lionel Robbins, who Keynes characterized as supporting the view that economics is a natural science (*CW*, XIV, p. 297). Robbins, of course, is especially well known for his *An Essay on the Nature and Significance of Economic Science* argument that interpersonal comparisons of utility are inappropriate in economics if economics is to be regarded as a science (1935; 1938). For Robbins, interpersonal utility comparisons essentially depend upon value judgements, and value judgements, in contrast to judgements of a factual nature, are not verifiable and thus not scientific (1935, pp. 148–9). Robbins's critique had a dramatic impact on economists when it appeared, since it created significant doubts among economists concerning the legitimacy of redistributive social welfare policies, which had been standard in economics since Marshall. Indeed, Robbins's argument was an important stimulus to Roy Harrod's Presidential Address to Section F of the British Association, 'Scope and Method of Economics', which was published in the September 1938 *Economic Journal*. Keynes's own remarks about Robbins and economics came in correspondence with Harrod prior to the latter's August presentation of the Address. Robbins also responded to Harrod in a December 1938 *Economic Journal* comment.

Accordingly, that Keynes argued that economics is a moral science, and that it justifiably employs introspection and judgements of value (or value judgements), should be taken to stand in direct opposition to Robbins's position. In claiming one can consult one's own imagined reaction to given circumstances, and then analogically assess the motives and intentions of economic agents whose behaviour is to be explained, Keynes confronts essentially the same issues that Robbins addressed in arguing against interpersonal utility comparisons. Moreover, it might well be said that the focus of the issue for Keynes – as clearly it is for Robbins – is whether it is methodologically reasonable to make value judgements in economics, since Keynes allows that introspection also involves judgements of value, when one assesses the strength or force of a presumed motive ascribed to a given economic agent analogically from one's own case. How, then, might Keynes have justified his proposed reliance on judgements of value (or value judgements) in light of Robbins's assertion that such judgements cannot be scientific?

First, Keynes, from the time of his 1904 'Ethics in Relation to Conduct' critique of Moore's reliance on the frequency theory of probability, clearly believed that the evidence potentially favourable to a given proposition always requires interpretation. This implies that individual judgement is indispensable to empirical argument, and also that judgements of value are involved in an investigator's assessment of the quality and significance of evidence at hand. On this view, Robbins's model of an *a posteriori* verification of empirical propositions – where the facts effectively speak for themselves – misrepresents scientific practice, since empirical verification lacks the exceptional standing claimed for it and does not offer a clear methodological alternative to using judgements of value. Second, however, Keynes unlike Robbins, believed that judgements of value could be reasonably objective, and that this provided positive justification for their (selective) use in economics. Keynes early on argued, in his 'Miscellanea Ethica' paper, that a reapplication of Moore's organic unities principle made it possible to ground moral judgements more securely than Moore had done in his *Principia Ethica*, and thus that moral judgements could generally be thought objective. This conclusion was supported by Keynes's distinction between what one actually thinks and feels and what one ought to think and feel. Although certainly it is not always straightforward how these are distinguished, nonetheless in Keynes's view there is a difference between them. In contrast, it is fair to say that from Robbins's point of view, judgements of value are invariably associated with what individuals happen to think and feel, since there is no agreed-upon manner – no method of verification – in which one can say how one ought to think and feel.

Indeed, it is the willingness or unwillingness to claim that a genuine difference exists between what one actually thinks and feels and what one ought to think and feel that separates the respective positions of Robbins and Keynes on the use of introspection as a methodological strategy in economics. Robbins, in his critique of interpersonal utility comparisons, argued that there was no means of testing the magnitude of one individual's satisfaction derived from a given income as compared with that of another, and that the effort to do this inevitably necessitated value judgements.

> Introspection does not enable A to measure what is going on in B's mind, nor B to measure what is going on in A's. There is no way of comparing the satisfaction of different people (Robbins, 1935, p. 139).

Keynes, however, did not associate scientificity exclusively with verification through measurement, and thus did not regard the lack of measurability and the attendent recourse to value judgement in introspection as an indication of non-objective judgement.[5] In part, he believed this because he believed value judgements could be objective in the sense of it being possible to say what an individual ought to think and feel in given circumstances, so that it was not necessary for example, as Robbins thought, to say that one could never compare two individuals' satisfaction with a given income.

As a methodological approach, accordingly, introspection depends upon defending the possibility of there being certain kinds of value judgements – namely, those that are objective in the sense of being intersubjectively defensible. To be able to consult one's own imagined reaction to circumstances experienced by others, and treat this projected response as informative about others' motives and intentions, one must be able to say with confidence that, since individuals ought generally to be expected to respond to such circumstances in certain ways, one's own projected response in a situation can be thought representative of those of others. This is, as noted above in connection with Keynes's discussion of 'the approximate uniformity of human organs', a matter of having some methodological foundation for explaining the intersubjective side of human judgement to accompany his attention to individual judgement. Both, it was argued, are necessary to an account of the representative individual employed in introspective analogical reasoning, since the individual consulting his or her own case must be both distinct and typical of those whose behaviour is observed. Robbins, unlike Keynes, was reluctant to attribute 'an approximate uniformity of human organs' to individuals, and thus a capacity in judgement to individuals whereby economists' introspective judgements of others' thoughts and feelings could be thought legitimate. In effect, Robbins, saw but one dimension to human nature – namely, that especially subjective side that Keynes associated with the capacity for a distinctively individual judgement, and which is today associated with the complete exogeneity of taste.

CONCLUSION

Keynes's moral science view of economics has received little attention, no doubt due in part to the inaccessibility of its philosophical foundations, but also undeniably to the modern trend in methodological thinking that treats economics as what Keynes termed for Robbins a natural science. Keynes's understanding, however, is provocative, in that it links this methodological conception to fundamental questions concerning the theory of the individual in economics. That is, since Keynes's implicit defence of introspection and judgements of value is rooted in a dual nature theory of the individual, the question naturally arises whether a justifiable commitment to this methodological approach entails a revision of economists' theory of the individual economic agent. In the discussion here, it should be emphasized, the plausibility of the more controversial component of Keynes's view – 'the approximate uniformity of human organs' – has not been assessed. Nor, moreover, has the relationship between individual judgement and an intersubjectively objective human judgement been explored in a manner that provides much more than an introduction to the idea of the representative individual. These further investigations, nonetheless, are arguably central to an understanding of not just Keynes's methodological views, but, more importantly, to an understanding of his theoretical strategies concerning the independent variables, 'in the first instance', of *The General Theory* – the propensity to consume, the marginal efficiency of capital schedule and the rate of interest (VII, p. 245). Accordingly, further investigation of these questions must necessarily take as its reference point the logic of the theory of the individual.

NOTES

1. Permission to quote from unpublished manuscripts in the J.M. Keynes Papers in King's College Library was kindly granted by King's College, Cambridge University. Unpublished writings of J.M. Keynes © The Provost and Scholars of King's College, Cambridge, 1991.
2. Compare, for example, J.N. Keynes's remarks about introspection (1955, p. 173).
3. This seems to be Lionel Robbins's position, discussed below.
4. The two passages from Keynes's unpublished writings quoted in the text are from 'Miscellanea Ethica'.
5. For Keynes's views on measurement of probabilities, see O'Donnell (1989).

7. The Methodology of the Critique of the Classical Theory: Keynes on Organic Interdependence

Anna Carabelli

KEYNES'S METHODOLOGICAL CRITIQUE OF THE CLASSICAL THEORY

The traditional approach to Keynes's critique of the classical theory has been that of stressing its contents. Here I approach it from a different perspective, by trying to show the methodological ground upon which this critique – in line with his own approach to economic theory – was based.[1]

For this reason I reconstruct Keynes's 'methodology of criticism' (as I call this new perspective), avoiding any reference – so far as is possible – to the aspects of *content*. I wish to show that the latter, albeit quite fundamental in supplying the ammunition for Keynes's main attack on the classical theory, were not its only main instruments.

The importance of this perspective for understanding his own approach to economic theory, has been pointed out by Keynes himself in different parts of his writings. As far as *The General Theory* is concerned, let us consider what he wrote in its various Prefaces. In the 13 December 1935 Preface, he wrote: 'I have thought it important, not only to explain my own point of view, but also to show in what it departs from the prevailing theory' (*CW*, VII, p. xxi). Again the crucial role was restressed in the Preface to the German Edition (7 September 1936): 'My emphasis ... upon the point of my divergence from received doctrine' (*CW*, VII, p. xxv). And, finally, this was restressed in the Preface to the French edition, 20 February 1939: 'what I regard as the main *differentiae* of my approach' (*CW*, VII, p. xxxii). He wrote this, after having pointed out in the same Preface, that 'its method' and, in particular, 'its presuppositions' had remained the same for a century (*CW*, VII, p. xxxi).

In particular, it should be noted that Keynes tackled this aspect right at the beginning of the *General Theory*, in its first two chapters. The main argument presented in Chapter 1 – which is only half a page long – focused on the need for a methodological criticism, stating that the choice of the title of the book (and of course not only that) was 'to contrast the character of my arguments and conclusions with those of the *classical* theory' (*CW*, VII, p. 3; see also p. 257). Furthermore, Chapter 2 and the appendix to Chapter 19 of the General Theory were fully oriented towards a methodological critique.

THE PREVIOUS CRITICS

Keynes considered the classical theory to be quite strong and realized that it was not easy to criticize, since, despite repeated past criticism it had resisted quite well and for quite a long time. Indeed, he considered it a well structured theory, which did not present, at first sight, apparent errors. The strength of the orthodox classical theory lay in its being a well organized system of thought and doctrines which had acquired consensus through persuasion and through its ability to convince. Due to this consensus it had then (in Keynes's time) completely penetrated habitual modes of thought. In 'Poverty in plenty: is the economic system self-adjusting?' (1934), Keynes wrote:

> The strength of the self-adjusting school depends on its having behind it almost the whole body of organised economic thinking and doctrine of the last hundred years. This is a formidable power. It is the product of acute minds and has persuaded and convinced the great majority of the intelligent and disinterested persons who have studied it.... For it lies behind the education and the habitual modes of thought, not only of economists, but of bankers, business men and civil servants and politicians of all parties (XIII, pp. 488–9).

Its power as a tool of thought also lay in this strength, even though it led to conclusions which to Keynes, seemed unacceptable on common-sense grounds. Keynes wrote that classical theory 'reached conclusions quite different from what the ordinary uninstructed person would expect' and that it created 'a cleavage between the conclusion of economic theory and those of common sense' (VII, pp. 33, 350).

Of course, Keynes was aware that, before his attempt, many thinkers had tried to criticize the classical theory. Thus, it will be interesting to consider what methodological errors Keynes attributed to the preceding opponents of the classical theory – errors on which he blamed their unsuccessful criticism and which he did not want to repeat. As a result of this investigation (a sort of criticism of criticism!), we will learn what, according to Keynes, *not* to do when criticizing a theory.

Let us see, first, when and where the classical theory was, according to Keynes, attacked; second, the errors made by the preceding opponents; and, third, the reasons given by Keynes for its resistance to those attacks.

The opponents considered by Keynes were the authors he called the 'brave army of heretics' (*CW*, VII, p. 371). He distinguished between the old and the new heretics, convinced that the latter – 'the heretics of today' as he called them – were 'the descendants of a long line of heretics' (*CW*, XIII, p. 488). Among them Keynes listed Mandeville, Malthus, Marx, Hobson and Mummery, Gesell, Major Douglas, Dalton, Drage, Wootton (see *CW*, VII, pp. 353–8, 370–1; *CW*, XIII, pp. 487–8).

Keynes thought that their criticism of the classical theory had been empiricist rather than rationalist. These critics believed, according to Keynes, that mere observation was sufficient to show that facts did not conform to the orthodox conclusions and that mere observation could question a theory:

> The heretics of today ... are deeply dissatisfied. They believe that common observation is enough to show that facts do not conform to the orthodox reasoning (*CW*, XIII, pp. 488–9).

But, for Keynes, this could not be validated methodologically. Underlying this criticism was Keynes's own epistemological approach to the relationship between theory and observation, manifested in *A Treatise on Probability*. Observation was, for him, theory-laden (*TP*, *CW*, VIII, p. 231; see also Carabelli 1988, pp. 69–71).[2] How could it raise doubt on something upon which it was grounded? Mere empirical criticism based upon the observations of facts which were in contrast with the conclusions of the theory was therefore useless as a critique of a theory. As a consequence, the mere pointing out that facts (empirical events) did not conform to the orthodox reasoning was bound to be unsuccessful as a critique.[3]

Keynes – in contrast to the heretics' empiricist method – thought that logic, rather than mere observation, was the proper way to raise doubts about a theory.

Keynes included the German Economic School among this group of 'heretics'. In contrast with the theoretical attitude demonstrated by German thinkers in other disciplines (suffice to think of Keynes's own intellectual deference to German logicians in *A Treatise on Probability*), he accused the school of being 'sceptical, realistic', content with historical facts and results, or utilizing 'empirical methods' and discarding 'formal analysis' (*CW*, VII, p. xxv).

The second mistake detected by Keynes in the heretics' critique was related to the fact that, although rejecting the conclusions, they still accepted the premises of the classical theory. In 'Poverty in plenty', Keynes wrote: 'Indeed, many of them [the heretics] accept the orthodox premises' (*CW*, XIII, p. 489). So their critical position was, according to Keynes, inconsistent, as they supported right conclusions and wrong premises.[4] Thus, for this reason they were bound to be defeated and 'have made no impression on the citadel' (*CW*, XIII, p. 489). This criticism by Keynes shows clearly that the classical theory was seen by him as a coherent set of premises and derived conclusions.

THE POSITION OF KEYNES'S CONTEMPORARIES

Keynes made an analogous criticism of incoherence against contemporary economists, particularly Henderson, Brand and Robbins (*CW*, XIII, pp. 487, 491), and also Pigou and Robertson.

Their approach was, according to him, even more ambiguous than that of the heretics, some of them even sharing the same incoherence:

> Post-war economists seldom ... succeed in maintaining this point *consistently*; for they thought to-day is too much permeated with the contrary tendency and with facts of experience too obviously inconsistent with their former view (*CW*, VII, p. 20).[5]

Others, although not explicitly sharing classical premises, accepted, according to Keynes, its conclusions:

> Contemporary economists, who might hesitate to agree with Mill, do not hesitate to accept conclusions which require Mill's doctrine as their premiss (*CW*, VII, p. 19).

Nevertheless, Keynes thought that both his contemporaries' and the old and new heretics' approach was to be considered inconsistent (either with their former view or with the premises of the classical theory) as, in particular, they failed to draw the due consequences from their methodological position. In fact, according to Keynes, none of them realized that the rejection of the classical theory's conclusions called for a revolution in economic theory:

> But they have not drawn sufficiently far-reaching consequences; and have not revised their fundamental theory (*CW*, VII, p. 20; also *CW*, XIV, p. 79).

A consequence of this was a carelessness in the formulation of the alternative theory, and – even when actually advancing an alternative theory – they fell into a third type of error, termed by Keynes 'incompleteness of theory' (*CW*, VII, p. 370; also pp. 340, 350, 355–6, 368–70).

THE REASONS GIVEN BY KEYNES FOR THE PREVIOUS CRITICS' ERRORS

The fundamental error Keynes attributed to the previous and to some contemporary critics of the orthodox theory was to accept the premises and to attack the conclusions. How could these critics mix these two levels of reasoning within the classical theory without realizing it was inconsistent? Paradoxically, they started from wrong premises and reached right conclusions. What were the reasons for such an inconsistency on their part? Keynes thought that their refusal of the classical theory's conclusions depended more on flair, instinct, practical good sense and experience of the world, rather than on logic. In 'Poverty in plenty', he wrote:

> They propose remedies prompted by instinct, by flair, by practical good sense, by experience of the world – half-right, most of them, and half-wrong... Indeed, many of them accept the orthodox premises; and it is only because their flair is stronger than their logic that they do not accept its conclusions (*CW*, XIII, pp. 488–9).

It is true that, in *A Treatise on Probability*, Keynes did not strictly separate logic from flair, instinct and so on but, equally, he considered mere flair without logic (as well as logic without flair) sterile.[6] He felt that it was logic which was needed in order to demolish a theory and to attack it at 'the citadel':

Thus, if the heretics on the other side of the gulf are to demolish the forces of nineteenth century orthodoxy ... they must attack them in their citadel. No successful attack has yet been made (*CW*, XIII, pp. 488–9).

So Keynes sided with 'those standing on [his] side of the gulf, whom ... [he] ventured to describe as half-right and half-wrong' – that is, with the heretics (*CW*, XIII, p. 490) on the basis of their right conclusions, although he did not accept their wrong premises, which were the same as those of the classical theory. In 'Poverty in plenty', he wrote:

Now I range myself with the heretics. I believe their flair and their instinct move them towards the right conclusions. But I was brought up in the citadel and I recognise its power and might (*CW*, XIII, pp. 488–9).

Dissatisfied with the methodological standard of their criticism, he wanted to locate and identify the flaw in the classical theory. Again, in 'Poverty and plenty', he wrote:

For me ... it is impossible to rest satisfied until I can put my finger on the flaw in that part of the orthodox reasoning which leads to the conclusions which for various reasons seem to me to be inacceptable (*CW*, XIII, p. 489).

Logic – rather than empiricism, instinct, flair, experience of the world and practical good sense – was the instrument of thought necessary to criticize classical theory.

THE 'RIGHT' CRITIQUE: CRITIQUE OF PREMISES

Keynes thought that the heretics' attitude was not only methodologically inconsistent but also 'ultimately dangerous' (*CW*, XIII, p. 492). Their mistake was even more troublesome given that Keynes thought – in contrast with the heretics' criticism – that the relationship between premises and conclusions in the classical theory was perfectly *consistent*. Keynes even stressed that the superstructure of the classical theory was built in a quite careful way: '...the superstructure [of the orthodox economics]... has been erected with great care for logical consistency' (*GT*, Preface, *CW*, VII, p. xxi; see also pp. 33, 192). So, if the fault of the classical theory did not lie either in the empirical unacceptability of conclusions or in the logical inconsistency between premises and conclusions, where did it lie? Keynes even affirmed that if the basic system of the classical theory was unassailable, as implied in the heretics' methodological attitude, then, consistently, one had to accept its conclusions (*CW*, XIII, p. 491).

But, according to Keynes, the classical system of thought *was* assailable and should be attacked at its heart. The flaw had to be somewhere the heretics had not looked. But where was this 'citadel' of the classical theory? Only a successful attack on it, given its 'power and might', could foster a revolution in theory (*CW*, XIII, p. 489; also p. 492).

For Keynes, the 'citadel' was obviously the premises of the classical theory, so the attack should be moved against the status of its premises, rather than against the conclusions or against the connection between premises and conclusions. This was the only route towards the much-needed theoretical change in economics.

Explicit and Tacit Assumptions

The flaw in the premises of the classical theory lay in the fact that the latter lacked 'clearness': 'For if orthodox economics is at fault, the error is to be found not in the superstructure ..., but in a lack of clearness ... in the premisses' (*GT, CW*, VII, p. xxi; also pp. 33, 192). This proved to be the right critique of the classical theory: finally, Keynes could put his 'finger on the flaw in that part of the orthodox reasoning which leads to the conclusions ... inacceptable' (*CW*, XIII, p. 489).

According to Keynes, the classical theory did not make explicit – as it should have done – some assumptions upon which its conclusions stood and upon which, as we will see later, depended the generality and the domain of validity of its arguments. These tacit assumptions were the most important, as they supported the conclusions of the classical theory. So, we can say that it is in this distinction that the *differentiae* between Keynes's and the classical theory's approach truly lies (*CW*, VII, p. xxxii). In the *General Theory* Keynes wrote on the role of tacit assumptions in facilitating the conclusions of the classical theory: 'granted this, all the rest follows' (*CW*, VII, p. 21).

As the conclusions of the classical theory – based upon those tacit assumptions – were perfectly logical, this led Keynes to think (in contrast to what was being advanced by the heretics) that the classical theory contained no logical inconsistency between premises and conclusions.[7] This was because tacit assumptions underlying the theory, made the relationship between premises and conclusions perfectly logical:

Thus writers in the classical tradition, overlooking the special assumption underlying their theory, have been driven inevitably to the conclusion, perfectly logical on their assumption that apparent unemployment ... must be due ... to a refusal by the unemployed factors to accept a reward which corresponds to their marginal productivity (*GT, CW,* VII, p. 16).

Search for the Tacit Assumptions

Keynes's search for the existence of the tacit assumptions in the classical theory permeated the whole of his writings. Here I wish to give just a few examples. In 1933, in his essay 'A Monetary Theory of Production', Keynes wrote of tacit assumptions:

> One of the chief causes of confusion lies in the fact that the assumptions of the real-exchange economy have been tacit, and you will search treatises on real-exchange economics in vain for any express statement of the simplifications introduced or for the relationship of its hypothetical conclusions to the facts of the real world (*CW,* XIII, p. 410).

In 1936, in the *General Theory*, he wrote:

> ...this strange supposition ...is what all members of the orthodox school are tacitly assuming....the classical school have slipt in an illicit assumption. For there may be *no* method available to labour as a whole ... (*CW,* VII, p. 13; see also p. xxv).

In 1939, in the Preface to the French Edition of the *General Theory*, Keynes restressed the point: 'Say was implicitly assuming that ...' (*CW,* VII, p. xxxv).[8]

However, it is interesting also to point out Keynes's criticism of Pigou, in the appendix to Chapter 19 of the *General Theory*, which is structured around the search for the existence of tacit assumptions in Pigou's theory (*CW,* VII, pp. 272–5). Let us look at the relevant opening passage:

> Since the tacit assumptions, which govern the application of the analysis, slip in near the outset of his argument, I will summarise his treatment up to the crucial point (*CW,* VII, p. 272; see also pp. 274–5 and 277).

Types of Tacit Assumptions

Once the existence of tacit assumptions in the classical theory has been shown, one can point out Keynes's care in detecting their different natures. The various assumptions considered by him can be classified in three types:

1. the assumption of independence from changes in the value of money;
2. the assumption of independence from changes in the value of output and unemployment;
3. the assumption of independence from changes in the level of income.

The assumption of independence from changes in the value of money carried with it the idea of neutral money and allowed the classical theoretician to pass, without any change in reasoning, from a real exchange economy to a money economy and brought with it the false analogy between the two. So, truly and consistently, by this assumption a money economy was equal to a real economy. According to Keynes, this assumption, within the classical theory, took different forms: that of neutral money, that of a uniform purchasing power of money (as if money were a 'mean sun') and that of neglecting possible changes in the general purchasing power of money.

Keynes took Marshall's and Pigou's writings into consideration with regard to this type of assumption. In Marshall, the assumption was introduced in the formulation of the theory of value, as if a theory of value could ignore changes in the value of money.[9] He noted that Marshall, in considering the theory of value, expressly stated that we may neglect possible changes in the general purchasing power of money. In particular, according to Keynes, Marshall supported Cournot's assumption of a standard of uniform purchasing power (*CW*, XIII, p. 409).

As regards Pigou, Keynes referred to his introduction of the tacit assumption that the supply of labour was independent of changes in the value of money (*CW*, XIII, pp. 409–10).

The assumption of independence from changes in the value of output and unemployment implied that the economic system was operating to its full capacity, which meant an independence from the level of output or of employment. According to the classical theory, its introduction allowed a straightforward transfer from a reasoning based upon a full-capacity economy to a reasoning based upon a situation characterized by unemployment.

In the Preface to the French Edition of the *General Theory*, written on 20 February 1939, Keynes suggested that the use of Say's basic assumptions, such as that demand is created by supply, meant independence from the level of output. The whole passage reads:

> J.B. Say...[has been] abandoned by most economists; but they have not extricated themselves from his basic assumptions and particularly from his fallacy that demand is created by supply... Say was implicitly assuming that the economic system was always operating up to its full capacity, so that a new activity was always in substitution for, and never in addition to, some other activity. Nearly all subsequent economic theory has depended on, in the sense that it has required, this same assumption (*CW*, VII, p. xxxv).

Equally, in Chapter 2 of the *General Theory*, the various tacit assumptions detected by Keynes in the classical theory of employment – which, as he wrote, all led back to one (*CW*, VII, pp. 21–2) – were simply the tacit assumption of independence from the level of output and employment.

Lastly, in the logical passage from an analysis at the individual level (either a single individual or a single industry or part) to one at community (whole or system) level, the introduction of the assumption of independence from changes in the level of income meant an independence of the analysis from changes in the level of community income. Thus, this crucial assumption allowed the mere transfer to the system as a whole of a type of reasoning which was only valid at individual level.

However, according to Keynes, when we move from individual level to community level, if the community income is not independent of the propensities of individuals to spend, this means that we cannot merely transfer the reasoning applied at the individual level to system level, without falling into logical paradoxes. What is independent at the individual level is not independent at the community level. In the actual reasoning of the classical theory, all this meant that the income of the system as a whole was taken as given.[10] This was quite clearly stated by Keynes in the Preface to the French edition of the *General Theory*:

> Quite legitimately we regard an individual's income as independent of what he himself consumes and invests. But this ...should not have led us to overlook the fact that the demand arising out of the consumption and investment of one individual is the source of the incomes of other individuals, so that incomes in general are not independent, quite the contrary, of the disposition of individuals to spend and invest (*CW*, VII, pp. xxxii–xxxiii; see also p. 21 and *CW*, XIII, p. 278).

The Characteristics of Classical Tacit Assumptions

The three types of tacit assumptions all came down to an assumption of 'logical independence from'. This meant that the classical theory was valid *always* and for *all* the (or for *any*) levels of the variables taken into consideration – that is, *always* and for *all* values of money, for *all* levels of output, for *all* levels of capacity, for *all* levels of employment, for *all* levels of income. All this amounted to saying that there was a characteristic common to the three classical tacit assumptions: the characteristic of universality in space and time.

The following passages show how Keynes pinpointed this common characteristic of universality – *always* and *for all* or *any* values or levels of the variables considered (money, income, output, capacity, employment). As to 'all', Keynes noted:

> The reader will remember that according to the classical theory, $\delta D_w = \delta N$ for *all* values of N [employment] (*CW*, XIII, p. 427, mid-1934 draft of Chapter 6 of the *General Theory*).

As to 'always', he noted in the 1939 Preface to the French edition of the *General Theory*:

> Say was implicitly assuming that the economic system was *always* operating up to its full capacity, so that a new activity was *always* in substitution for, and never in addition to, some other activity (*CW*, VII, p. xxxv, emphasis added).

And finally as to 'any' and 'always' together, he noted:

> The view that *any* increase in the quantity of money is inflationary ... is bound with the underlying assumption of the classical theory that we are *always* in a condition where a reduction in the real rewards of the factors of production will lead to a curtailment in their supply (*CW*, VII, p. 304).

From this we can derive:

1. that universality brought with it independence *always* and from *all* the values or levels of the variables considered;
2. that universality also presupposed the general validity of the classical premises.

'Always' and for 'all or any' levels and values of the variables meant validity *in general*, – that is, unlimited validity. So that this common characteristic of universality of the tacit assumptions of the classical theory also represented the domain of its validity.

The Limits Set to the Classical Tacit Assumptions

If these assumptions were truly universal as the classical theory tacitly supposed, then the classical theory was unassailable. If they were not, there was a way to criticize it.

Keynes maintained that, within the classical theory, its validity implicitly referred to all the levels or values of the variables considered and to any circumstances, but he did not think that this assumption of universality was true.

He wanted to show that the tacit conditions of the classical theory were extremely limited in terms of validity (*CW*, VII, p. 378).[11] In particular, the consequence of the fact that the assumptions of independence were not true *always* and for *all* the values or levels of the variables considered was that the validity of its premises was limited to *some* particular values or levels of the variables considered and to *some* particular moments in time, circumstance or context. A very strong limitation for a theory!

As regards Keynes's discussion of the limiting conditions of the assumption of independence from changes in the value of money – that is, the classical assumption of the neutrality of money – one can recall what he wrote in 'A Monetary Theory of Production' (1933):

> We are not told what conditions have to be fulfilled if money is to be neutral. Nor is it easy to supply the gap. Now the conditions required for the 'neutrality' of money, ...are ... precisely the same as those which will insure that crises *do not occur*. If this is true, the real exchange economics ... is a singularly blunt weapon for dealing with the problem of booms and depressions. For it has assumed away the very matter under investigation (*CW*, XIII, pp. 410–11).

And, as regards the level of output, Keynes in the mid-1934 draft of Chapter 6 of the *General Theory* showed that the assumptions of the classical theory referred *not* to *all* levels but to only *one* level of the variable. He wrote:

> Its significance [of the then purely negative innovation of Keynes's theory]...will depend on our establishing our contention that there is, in

general, only *one* level of output at which equality holds between marginal prime cost and the anticipated price, so that under competition the aim of maximising profit will cause entrepreneurs to chose that level of employment for which this equality holds. Only if the equality held good, as the classical theory assumes, for *all* levels of output, would it be true that there is nothing to check the increase of employment... (*CW*, XIII, p. 427, emphases added).

So, the 'lack of clearness in the premises' meant a lack in their generality and consequently in the conclusions of the classical theory(*CW*, VII, p. xxi). It meant that there were premises or assumptions which were implicit in the classical arguments which – having limits of generality and of validity – also set limits to the classical conclusions, thereby limiting the generality of that theory. In fact, their limited generality and validity reduced the classical theory to a specific case of a more general theory.[12]

What Keynes Meant by a 'General' Theory

Now we can also grasp the true meaning of the word 'general' which baffles the reader of the *General Theory* as soon as he reads its title. In Chapter 1 of the *General Theory*, Keynes wrote:

> I have called this book the *General Theory of Employment, Interest and Money* placing the emphasis on the prefix *general*. The object of such a title is to contrast the character of my arguments and conclusions with those of the *classical* theory (CW, VII, p. 3).

For Keynes, a general theory was one which did not tacitly introduce hypotheses of 'independence from'.[13] Thus, his use of the word 'general' is truly connected with his methodological criticism of the classical theory. In it lay the contrast between the 'character' of Keynes's argument and that of the classical theory (*CW*, VII, p. 3; see also p. 276).

A theory which, at the beginning of its analysis, avoided introducing limiting assumptions of independence, was truly general. Theories – like the classical theory – which did not were simply special cases of the former:

> We are thus led to a more *general* theory, which includes the classical theory with which we are familiar, as a special case (*CW*, VII, pp. xxii–xxiii; see also XIII, p. 420).

The Logical Flaw in the Classical Theory: *Ignoratio Elenchi*

To understand the contrast between a general theory and one of its cases, we must point out that the mistake Keynes attributed to the introduction of the tacit assumptions by the classical theory is one of the standard mistakes described in classical logic. Keynes referred to it as *ignoratio elenchi* (*CW*, VII, p. 259).[14]

This brought the logical reasoning of the classical theory to a 'false inference', a 'fallacy of composition', an 'optical illusion, which makes two essentially different activities appear to be the same', a 'false analogy', a 'paradox': that is, the transfer, without changes, of an analysis applied to one part of a system to the system as a whole (*CW*, XIII, p. 278; *CW*, VII, p. xxxii, 20–21),[15] or, synonymously, to the mistaken 'idea that it is comparatively easy to adapt the hypothetical conclusions of a real wage economics to the real world of monetary economics' (*CW*, XIII, p. 410; see also p. 278).

In particular, the mistake attributed to the classical theorists was to ignore the dependence of the system as a whole on changes in the variables considered, or to ignore the relevance for the system as a whole of the *changes* in the variables (which, as we shall see, is the same thing).[16]

The Epistemological Role of Classical Tacit Assumptions

It is clear at this point that the nature of the criticism which Keynes made of the premises of the classical theory was not concerned with their empirical relevance. It was truly a criticism of logical relevance.[17]

Now we will see what this involves from an epistemological point of view. As noted, the three tacit assumptions all came down to the introduction of an assumption of 'logical independence from'. In Keynes's specific case, 'logical relevance/irrelevance' and 'logical dependence/ independence' were exactly equal concepts: they play a central role in Keynes's epistemology, as advanced in *A Treatise on Probability*, in particular as to the notions of causality and the 'atomic hypothesis'. In fact, in *A Treatise on Probability*, a judgement of independence ('independence for knowledge') was deemed truly a judgement of logical irrelevance.[18] And the judgement of independence was at the basis of the acceptance by mathematical probability theory of a specific hypothesis on the atomic nature of the variables considered (*CW*, VIII, p. 276–8; see also Carabelli 1988: Chapter 6).

In the classical economic theory, the assumption of independence from', first meant logical 'irrelevance' (of changes in the value of money, in the level of output and in the level of income). A direct consequence of this irrelevance was, as we have seen, the implicit generality of the premises – always and for all levels or values of the variables. But it also meant – in a way very similar to that of the mathematical theory of probability – the implicit introduction of the 'atomic hypothesis', with all its quantitative and measurable attributes (numerical measurability, divisibility, time-reversibility, homogeneity, exhaustivity, completeness, permanent forces and primary qualities).

In the classical theory the tacit hypothesis of 'independence from' not only played the same epistemological role as the 'atomic hypothesis' in the mathematical theory of probability, but it also had a similar role to that played by the axiom of parallels in Euclidean geometry: 'It is, then, the assumption...which is to be regarded as the classical theory's "axiom of parallels"'. Once this assumption was introduced – in a way very similar to that of the introduction of the axiom of parallels in Euclidean geometry – a series of conclusions emerged automatically: 'granted this', wrote Keynes, 'all the rest follows' (*CW*, VII, p. 21; see also p. 16).

Complex Systems: Organic Interdependence

The introduction of the hypothesis of independence by the classical theory allowed it to deal with systems as if they were *always* isolable from *all* the levels or values of the variables considered. So, in introducing this assumption, the classical theory was really trying to isolate the economic system from changes in some variables – that is, to abstract from variability – a process which Keynes considered inapplicable to those systems with which economics dealt (or should deal) (*CW*, VII, p. xxxii; see also *CW*, V, p. 77).

In other words, the classical theory's assumption of independence was equal to an ungrounded assumption of isolability – an assumption which was very similar to one introduced in classical Newtonian physics. Thanks to this, the classical theory could speak of an economic individual, an industry or an economic system, each *in isolation*. In fact, economic individuals, industries and systems in isolation all behave similarly; and it should be emphasized that even isolable systems behave as if they were individuals or parts of systems. They are in fact systems in which some assumptions of independence allow their separation from changes in some other variables judged irrelevant. They are *simple* or *closed* systems in which the functional relationships among the variables are atomic in character.

In contrast to these simple systems stand non-isolable systems, which are truly *complex* or *open*. Given the general impossibility of separating them from changes in some other variables, the functional relationships among the variables in these systems are organic in character. 'Non-independence from' means that there is an organic interrelation among the variables under consideration.

It was in the latter systems that Keynes was mainly interested. We can now see that a general theory was, for Keynes, really a 'complex' theory – a theory where the non-independence from the variables considered meant that there was organic interdependence among them.[19]

CONCLUSION

We can therefore conclude that the main standpoint for Keynes's methodology of criticism of the classical theory was provided by the concept of organic interdependence – a concept which was at the base of his own positive approach to economics (his notion of 'macro' came from here!) and stemmed directly from his approach to probability.[20]

Certainly such a complex and open economic theory dominated by organic interdependence was very difficult for a theorist to cope with; suffice to consider the problems it raised in the exposition of the *General Theory*.[21] Tackling these problems is another task.

NOTES

1. The references to Keynes's writings are to *The Collected Writings of J.M. Keynes* (*CW*). On Keynes's methodological approach to economic theory, see Carabelli, (1988).
2. On observation, see Shapere (1982) and Hacking (1983, ch. 10).
3. It is interesting to consider Keynes's criticism of Malthus's approach. The methodological positions of Keynes and Malthus are commonly thought to have been similar, although this seems open to controversy. Actually, in the *General Theory*, Keynes criticized Malthus for his empiricist criticism of Ricardo and for the 'incompleteness' of the alternative theory advanced (*CW*, VII, p. 32).

    In contrast with this position, what emerges from Keynes's 'Essay on Malthus' and his 'Allocution', is a far less linear position. In these writings, Keynes's attitude towards Malthus's approach exhibited three main methodological shades, broadly corresponding to the three main phases of Malthus's intellectual life – that is, to the latter's three main groups of writings. Keynes considered Malthus's first work, *Essay on Population, a priori* and philosophical in method. On the other hand, he regarded its later editions as being characterized by a change in method: a change towards mere empiricism. This represented Malthus's second phase: the general principles were, according to Keynes, overwhelmed with 'inductive verifications' and reduced to 'simple generalisations' out of facts (*CW*, X, pp. 85–6). Finally, Keynes's approach to Malthus's more mature writings (in particular *An Investigation of the Cause of the Present High Price of Provisions* (1800) and the correspondence with Ricardo) brings to light aspects which, in my view, tend to outline Keynes's own approach more than Malthus's. In fact, the last part of Keynes's 'Essay on Malthus' and the whole 'Allocution' (*CW*, X, pp. 71–103, 104–8) have a flavour very similar to that created by Keynes in his well known reinterpretation of Newton's method, 'Essay on Newton, the Man', which stressed the mixture of formal thought and intuition necessary to 'understand' the 'complex confusion of the world of daily events', the 'unusual combination of keeping an open mind to the shifting picture of experience and of constantly applying to its interpretation the principle of formal thought', the grasping of 'what should be for an economist the relation of experience to theory' (*CW*, X, pp. 88, 107–8; on Newton see *CW*, X, especially p. 364; on Keynes's interpretation of Newton's method and the parallel with Keynes's own method, see Parsons, 1985 and Carabelli 1988, p. 109).

4.   On Marx's methodological position, Keynes maintained that Marx accepted Ricardian premises, so he criticized him of incoherence. In fact, he wrote about the 'Ricardian foundations of marxism' (*CW*, XIII, p. 493). On Keynes's criticism of the methodology of contemporary labourists, see Carabelli (1987).

5.   The most striking example among them was Pigou. He shared with Keynes a common attitude to practice and economic policy. Evidence for this agreement is *The Times* 1932 and 1933, where both Keynes and Pigou signed joint letters advocating countercyclical fiscal policy (*CW*, XXI, pp. 126, 137–40). On this, see Moggridge (1988, pp. 54–5). But also note Keynes's remark, made as late as October 1937, commenting on Pigou's *Socialism versus Capitalism* (1937):

> As in the case of Dennis [Robertson], when it comes to practice, there is really extremely little between us. Why do they insist on maintaining theories from which their own practical conclusions cannot possibly follow? It is a sort of Society for the preservation of Ancient Monuments (*CW*, XIV, p. 259).

6.   What Keynes meant by logic has previously been tackled in Carabelli (1982a, 1982b, 1985, 1988, especially ch. 8). He saw logic as ordinary language logic rather than formal logic, characterized by contingent reason seen as reasonableness relative to cognitive circumstances. It was nearer to a logic of opinion than a logic of truth. This interpretation of Keynes's view of logic (and of rationality) is in contrast with that advanced by O'Donnell (1982 and 1989a especially pp. 34, 38, 47, 90, 93, 97–8, although there are changes in attitude on this point between the 1989a and the 1982 versions), Lawson (1987, p. 961–3 and 1989, pp. 244–8) and Fitzgibbons (1988, pp. 26–8, 85). In pointing out Keynes's interests in universal truth and absolute knowledge, these authors tend more to stress Keynes's borrowings from Moore (for example, his Platonic realist view of the realm of abstract entities) and from Russell (for example, his view of formal logic) than his differences from them. On the contrary, I think that it is more important to grasp Keynes's novel approach in *A Treatise on Probability* by detecting their differences than to note their similarities. Elsewhere I tried to show how Keynes

attempted to abandon Moore's absolute and universal Platonism and Russell's view of formal logic. Here I would like to re-emphasize only a few points.

As in the Platonic tradition, Keynes considered logical relations as real objects (objective relations), but no longer on the basis of the spaceless and timeless immanent metaphysical reality with its static and universal *a priori* categories of infallible intuition and understanding. He tried to overcome the limits of universalistic abstractions which tend to eliminate from theoretical concern that which is unique, contingent, changeable, space- and time-dependent. Furthermore, he did not accept the one-dimensional reality and the fact that concepts are permanently fixed – that is, the two conditions required by absolute metaphysical realism. For Keynes, both thought and reality were multidimensional. Theoretical categories were neither passively dictated (in a Platonic way) from an immutable theory-independent reality, nor freely imposed (in a Kantian way) aprioristically once and for all upon reality. Keynes, in my view, tried to cut through this dichotomy, as well as through many other positivist dichotomies. For him, there was no universal and absolute theoretical point of view – neither Platonic metaphysical realism nor Kantian transcendental subjectivity. Theoretical categories were therefore selective. On the basis of what theorists already actually know of, or about, reality, they have to choose (making explicit the reasons for the choice) a specific relevant point of view in the contingent cognitive circumstances in which they act. Making models of a changing reality (or introducing theoretical abstraction which is the same thing) is an art which cannot be universal. Equally, making it relative to changing cognitive circumstances does not mean that it is not real and objective, given the circumstances unless, of course, one automatically associates objectivity with universality and absoluteness, which Keynes did not. Actually, Keynes's criticism on universality and absoluteness raised against Moore and Russell was, similarly, later raised against classical economists. On this aspect, see also note 18 dealing with Keynes' notion of logical relevance.

In my view of Keynes's logic, in *A Treatise on Probability*, following Aristotle rather than Plato, he was interested in developing a contingent form of non-demonstrative reasoning (contingent reason) relative to contexts of shifting reality ('an open mind to the shifting picture of experience') in which things change rather than endure (Carabelli, 1988, pp. 126, 149–50, 279). In this context, rationality of variable and contingent experience lacks ontological constancy as well as *a priori* necessity. At the time of writing *A Treatise on Probability* Keynes was dissatisfied with the contemporary status of epistemology which was unable to deal with these aspects. One of the main characteristics of his methodological approach to probability was his (not always successful) attempt to cut through the positivist dichotomies: rationalism/empiricism, rationality/irrationality, science/art, science/ethics, theory/experience, mind/reality, primary/secondary qualities and so on. Certainly, he would have appreciated the current epistemology of complexity advanced by thinkers like Morin (1977–86, 1984, 1985), Prigogine (1980) and Nicolis (1986). On Keynes's view of logic which is close to that advanced here, see Dow (1988, p. 104).

7. It should be clear by now that logical consistency between premises and conclusions was no guarantee for Keynes that methodological errors had been avoided (see *CW*, VII, p. 371).

8. See also *CW*, VII, pp. 350, 364. Keynes's attitude here towards the search for tacit assumptions in theories and his attempt to make them explicit, showing their limits of validity, were not new. We find the same practice in *A Treatise on Probability* as far as the mathematical theory of probability, Bernoulli's principle of indifference, induction and statistical inference were concerned. See, for example, on Bernoulli's principle: 'They [these considerations] have only served

to make explicit what was always implicit in the principle [of indifference]' (*TP*, *CW*, VIII, p. 66; on this attitude, see also Carabelli, 1988, pp. 75, 267–8). Favereau (1985, p. 39) calls this attitude, 'l'hypothèse Wittgenstein', stressing the modernity of Keynes's epistemological approach in his attempt to show the limits of validity of a formal system ('the limits of a formal language'). As this attitude was not at all peculiar to Keynes's approach in the *The General Theory*, as Favereau suggests, I would call it 'l'hypothèse Keynes'.

9. According to Keynes, the theory of value was to be formulated, in contrast to the classical theory's view, in money terms. (See Chapters 4 and 21 of the *General Theory*, especially pp. 41, 293–4). On Keynes's earlier attitudes towards a money theory of value, see his essay, on 'The Economic Consequences of W. Churchill' (*CW*, IX, especially pp. 208–9 – this point is stressed by Wells, 1986, pp. 12–14) and in A Treatise on Money (*CW*, V, pp. 120–4, 137, 149–53). See also Rotheim (1981), Chick (1985), Weeks (1988), and my note 10.

10. Upon this was grounded Keynes's criticism that the classical saving and investment schedules could not 'shift independently of one another' and that there was interdependence between the two (*CW*, VII, p. 179). Equally, supply and demand curves for loanable funds were not independent. One 'could not obtain a determinate conclusion without introducing some additional equation or datum' (*CW*, XXIX, p. 228). Keynes linked the interdependence of supply and demand with his theory of value (*CW*, VII, pp. xxii–xxiii). Surrey (1988, pp. 110–13) suggests that at the heart of Keynes's criticism on the non-independence of classical supply and demand schedules lay a problem of systematic under-identification at the macro level by the classical method of analysis.

11. *The General Theory* was addressed to 'his fellow economists' and had as a principal object the study of 'difficult questions of theory', towards the aim of 'persuading economists to re-examine critically certain of their basic assumptions' (*CW*, VII, Preface, p. xxi).

12. A very similar criticism based on the tacit introduction of assumptions of independence had already been raised by Keynes against the quantity theory of money in *A Tract on Monetary Reform* (1923):

> ...the [quantity] theory has often been expounded on the further assumption that a *mere* change in the quantity of the currency cannot affect k, r, and k' – that is to say, in mathematical parlance, that *n* is an *independent variable* in relation to these quantities. It would follow from this that an arbitrary doubling of *n*, since this in itself is assumed not to affect k, r, and k', must have the effect of raising p to double what it would have been otherwise...Now 'in the long run' this is probably true... But this *long run* is a misleading guide to current affairs. In *the long run* we are all dead ... In actual experience, a change of n is liable to have a reaction both on k and k' and on r (*CW*, IV, p. 65).

Similar were his criticisms on the theory of purchasing power parity ('the theory requires a further assumption for its validity') and on the presumed intrinsic stability of the value of gold ('The *independent variety* of the influences determining the value of gold has been in itself a steadying influence ... The value of gold is no longer the resultant of the chance gifts of nature and the judgement of numerous authorities and individuals acting independently') (*CW*, IV, pp. 75, 133–4). In *A Treatise on Money* (1930), the point was re-emphasized: 'the purpose of isolating 'changes on the side of money'; 'subject to "independent" influences'; 'the non-independence of relative price changes' (*CW*, V, pp. 73, 75, 77).

13. A general theory in this sense – in contrast with the presuppositions of the classical theory – does not mean that it is also universal in time and space. For Keynes,

economic theory was a 'logic, a way of thinking', a 'method' (*CW*, XIV, p. 296; XII, p. 856) and, in particular, it was, as we have seen in note 7, a contingent form of non-demonstrative reasoning. Thus, a theory was general if it could cope with different hypothetical cases, characterized by different levels of dependence among the variables and permitted change and variability to play a central role in it. But the choice of the abstraction level of the theory, and therefore of the specific model among the possible ones applicable to practice, was not universal but relative to time and space circumstances. The ability to choose the specific model was described by Keynes as 'an art' (*CW*, XIV, p. 296). Obviously, the conclusions of the different models varied according to circumstance.

At this point it is also clear that Hayek's (1978, p. 287) definition of Keynes's general theory as 'scientistic' is ungrounded.

14. *Ignoratio elenchi* is one of the 13 types of fallacy of argument listed by Aristotle in *Sophistical Refutations* (1908 ed. by W.D. Ross, pp. 167a 20). The Latin title from the original Greek is *De Sophisticis Elenchis*). In this work Aristotle explicitly takes up the question of contentious reasoning. On this type of fallacy, see Hamblin (1970, pp. 31–2, 87–8).

15. In *A Treatise on Probability* Keynes referred to it as 'fallacy of independence' (*CW*, VIII, p. 191).

16. In logic, *ignoratio elenchi* is considered an informal fallacy of relevance. An informal fallacy is an error in reasoning not depending on the form of the argument but on its content. In particular, an informal fallacy of relevance occurs when the premises of an argument are irrelevant to, and incapable of, establishing the truth of the conclusion of an argument. Relevance implies that there should be some connection between the meanings of the premises and the conclusion of an argument. See Greenstein (1978, pp. 112, 132, 141) and Hamblin (1970, pp. 31–2). On Keynes's stress on the connection between relevance and meaning, see *TP*, *CW*, VIII, p. 62.

17. Thus, Keynes's criticism, even considering his remarks on classical hypothesis as 'inappropriate to facts' (*CW*, VII, p. 371), was not that the premises of the classical theory were either unrealistic or empirically irrelevant, but that they were not general ('lack ... of generality in the premisses', *CW*, VII, p. xxi) – that is, they were logically irrelevant and inadequate to the questions raised.

Keynes dealt with direct judgements of logical relevance in *A Treatise on Probability*, in his discussion of Bernoulli's principle of indifference (*CW*, VIII, pp. 58–60, 62, 113). Keynes there distinguished between judgements of preference or indifference and judgements of relevance of irrelevance. The first concern situations in which the evidence is the same but the conclusions are different; while the second concern situations in which the evidence is different but the conclusion is the same. Direct judgements of logical relevance concern, in particular, the effect that the probabilities of an argument are affected or not affected by the inclusion in the evidence of certain particular details. The effects of different amounts of relevant evidence (or of relevant knowledge as he also called it) were further discussed by him in dealing with the concept of the 'weight of argument' (*CW*, VIII, pp. 77–85).

For Keynes, judgements of logical relevance were not absolute, but were relative to the *quaesitum* and to the particular circumstances in which the latter was raised: in particular they were relative to 'some only of the known characteristics of the *quaesitum*, those characteristics ... which are *relevant* in the circumstances' (*CW*, VIII, p. 113; on relevance as adequacy and perspicuousness, see also Putnam, 1981, pp. 201–3). This notion was re-used by Keynes in *The General Theory*, in his choice of independent variables. The relativity was again stressed: 'in this place and context ... so little relevant ... on our *quaesitum*' (*CW*, VII, pp.

245, 247). And, as is well known, his 'object' of analysis was to discover what determined the level of output. Logical relevant factors were those which change fast and suddenly or those which could be managed for example, the rate of interest was judged as independent (*CW*, XXIX, p. 115).

Finally, it seems that this criticism by Keynes cannot be interpreted within the terms of the old and new polemics on the realism or instrumentalism of hypotheses of a theory or of one of its models (see Boland, 1989, ch. 4 and the bibliography there listed, but see also Morgenbesser, 1969; Nagel 1963; Mongin, 1988 and the following discussion in *Philosophy of Social Science*). Verification, confirmation, corroboration, falsification or just mere success in forecasting facts, played no role in Keynes's criticism of the classical theory's premises. So O'Donnell's (1989a, pp. 228–9) and Lawson's (1987 and 1989) emphasis on Keynes's empirical realism of hypotheses in contrast to instrumentalism seems misplaced. This type of polemics is internal within positivism. In brief, in the case of economics it was a polemics between Friedman and Samuelson. Keynes was already outside its terms. Further, so far as Lawson's two contributions are concerned, the author seems to mix two notions of realism (Platonic metaphysical realism and empirical realism) which I think are not so easily blended.

18. In *A Treatise on Probability*, Keynes decided to define independence by reference to the concept of logical relevance rather than to that of causality. The problem of the relation between logical relevance and empirical relevance – or material cause as he called it – he left unsolved (*CW*, VIII, pp. 182–3).

So, Keynes was not interested in material ontology – that is, how things are in reality – but in how things are actually *known* (or, rather, probably known) by us. The distinction he made was between '*causa essendi*' ('the cause why a thing is what it is') and '*causa cognoscendi*' ('the cause of our knowledge of the event') (*CW*, VIII, Note on the Use of the Term 'Cause', pp. 305–8). In this I disagree with Lawson's reading of Keynes as a 'realist', attempting 'to understand causal things and the ways in which they act' and 'to analyse causal structures at their own level of being' (Lawson, 1989, p. 239). Keynes considered cause a relative cognitive concept – that is, a logical ground or a reason for believing which is relative to particular circumstances (see the reference to 'causal analysis' as '*strictly logical*' in the 1933 draft of *The General Theory*, *CW*, XXIX, p. 73).

He therefore connected the concept of relevance with probable knowledge of or about things rather than with things in themselves. To clarify this point, see the following quotation from *A Treatise on Probability*:

…this conclusion cannot be reached unless *a priori* … we have some reason for thinking [i.e. *causa cognoscendi*] that there may be such a causal connection between the quantities [i.e. causa essendi] (*CW*, VIII, p. 466).

Relevance was connected with the first type of cause (that is, *causa cognoscendi*) not with the second (that is, *causa essendi*). On the connection between irrelevance and independence and on their role in Keynes's concept of *causa cognoscendi*, see Carabelli (1985, pp. 154, 157; 1988, sections 3.5, 3.6, and 6.1).

19. We can now also fully grasp Keynes's methodological criticism of Pigou. According to Keynes, Pigou was taking 'out of a complex system' two variables (employment and real wages) which were 'not' logically 'independent' (*CW*, XIII, pp. 312–13).

That *both* employment and real wage rates were functions of the level of effective demand – in particular an inverse relation not to be confused (according to Asimakopulos 1988, p. 79) with a demand curve for labour – was equally stressed by Keynes in the 1933 draft chapter of *The General Theory*: 'we may well discover empirically a correlation between employment and real wages. But this will occur, not because the one causes the other, but because both are consequences of the same cause' (*CW*, XXIX, p. 100). On this see also Brothwell (1988, p. 54).

20.   On the notion of organic interdependence, see *CW*, VIII, pp. 276–8. Recently attention has been paid by various authors to the centrality of this concept within Keynes's economic approach – albeit drawing different interpretations of its role. See Brown-Collier, 1985; Brown-Collier and Bausor, 1988; Davis, 1989 and 1991; Fitzgibbons, 1988, Lawson, 1989; O'Donnell, 1982 and 1989a; Winslow, 1986 and 1989; Carabelli, 1985 and 1988. An early contribution which pointed out the notion of open and complex systems in economics, but which, however, did not refer to Keynes, should also be mentioned: Grunberg, 1966 and 1978.

21.   Keynes thought that, in economics, coping with complexity could be done only by using ordinary language (which is an open language) rather than artificial closed languages like mathematics (*CW*, VII, p. 297). On this aspect, see Carabelli (1985 and 1988, pp. 141–4, 152–7). See also Walker (1985, p. 176), who disagrees with Keynes's idea that mathematics is linked to the atomistic hypothesis and is unable to deal with problems of organic unity. And see also Simon (1962) and Gottinger (1983) for attempts to cope with complexity in mathematical terms.

8. The Significance of Keynes's Idealism

Athol Fitzgibbons

INTRODUCTION

It is now clear that John Maynard Keynes's economics is part of a more comprehensive system with previously unsuspected philosophic roots, and that the *General Theory* in particular makes better sense when considered in terms of it. This wider system may appeal especially to economists who believe that Keynesianism embodies fundamental truths, even if it has partly lost its way.

Anyone who studies Keynes's own writings soon finds that his followers, including both the neo-Keynesians and the post-Keynesians, have reinterpreted the *General Theory*. Each school developed what it thought was a more rigorous approach in terms of its own methods and values. The neo-Keynesians built on Leon Walras and the post-Keynesians on Ricardo, basing their Keynesianism on the two greatest admirers of the method of natural science in economics. Although these 'bastard' systems emphasize the role of aggregate demand and contain other valuable insights, they fall short of Keynes's formulation of a 'moral science' of economics. They should not be regarded as consistent systems of thought, but need to be justified in terms of Keynes's own method.

For this reason a new wave of scholarship has become preoccupied with exegesis, regardless of the warnings against 'fundamentalist' interpretations of Keynes's original meaning. These warnings are valid to the extent that interpreting what Keynes really said is an imperfect art. It is subject to the same principles of probability that Keynes explored, and in according to the logic of his argument – that probability begins and ends with probability and not with truth – we will never discover what was the exact and pure Keynesian system. Nevertheless, and following

Keynes again, it is only sensible to say that some accounts of Keynes are extremely unlikely (especially given the misconceptions concerning his work) and it is helpful and meaningful to argue that one account is closer than any other.

Another reason for fundamentalism is that, despite their theoretical rigour, the models which built on Keynes left a great deal out. Some trenchant objections to Keynesianism apply not to Keynes's own system but to the technical or political orientation of his followers. At the theoretical level, Keynesianism is said to offer no account of probability or expectations. On the political right it is regarded as a socialist threat to liberty, while on the left it is regarded as devoid of any ethical vision. These objections are common currency, but they are hard to reconcile with the range of Keynes's philosophic interests.

Before he became an economist Keynes was a philosopher, whose *Treatise on Probability* was the 'first systematic work in English on the logical foundations of probability for fifty five years' (Braithwaite, 1973, p. xv). Keynes approached probability through the study of moral philosophy, in which subject he served a long apprenticeship as a follower of the idealist utilitarian, G.E. Moore. Keynes's probability and ethics underlay a political philosophy, sometimes regarded as a landmark in liberalism, which tried to reconcile a genuine idealism with the requirements of economic growth.

However, the analysis of Keynes's intellectual context is very new. Only in recent years have economists turned to the *Treatise on Probability* for a formal justification of the economics of uncertainty. It is now well known that some of Keynes's writings have not been published, including drafts of the *Treatise on Probability*, his early writings on ethics and his undergraduate essay on *The Political Philosophy of Edmund Burke*. The essential Keynesian theme can perhaps be derived from his better known writings, but these omissions are symptomatic of the narrow picture of Keynes that prevailed until recent years.

KEYNESIAN EXEGESIS

The new Keynesian exegesis began with biographers opening up a wide front while analysts were simultaneously looking for the methodological roots of Keynesianism. Biographies by Robert Skidelsky (1983) and Charles Hession (1984) showed that the 'one great book' approach is inconsistent with what we know of Keynes's intellectual orientation and life. To the extent that the biographers tried to derive an analytical account from the biographical material (Hession, 1984, pp. 108–9; Skidelsky, 1983, p. xvii), they were in error. Nevertheless they opened the debate by showing that previously neglected influences, including the liberating effect of Bloomsbury and of G.E. Moore, had to be accounted for in Keynes's system.

Yet the search for this wider system immediately leads to analytical complexities, particularly concerning the meaning which Keynes gives to the concept of reason. Whereas the *General Theory* is supposed to be about uncertainty and the unpredictable future, the *Treatise on Probability* is supposed to explain why, on the contrary, there *is* usually enough knowedge for rational action. If philosophers and economists had communicated they might well have identified a 'Keynes problem', analogous to the alleged 'Adam Smith problem' – a substantial inconsistency between the writer's philosophy and his economics.

Even if Keynesian economic theory is compared to his policy there seems to be a contradiction. Whereas Keynesian economic theory has been drawn from the *General Theory*, his economic policy followed the tradition associated with the *Treatise*: so Keynesian economic policy postulates central controllers who can partly anticipate the future, whereas

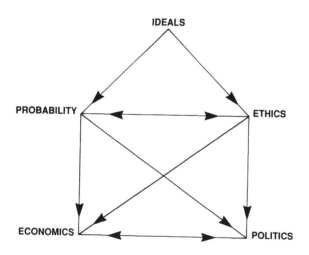

Figure 8.1   The single theme of Keynes's work

Keynesian economic theory postulates investors who have no foresight at all.

In *Keynes's Vision* I argued that there is no apostasy in Keynes's major works, but a single theme, varying in its application but constant in its essentials. The bare skeleton of that theme, indicating the cross-references between Keynes's economics and his philosophic and political ideas, is summarized in the schemata above (see Figure 8.1). The single arrows denote the direction of intellectual influence and the double arrows indicate a mutual compatibility of ideas.

As the illustration suggests, Keynes began from a metaphysical outlook which constituted the foundation of his thought. This overview was then transmitted into a philosophy of probability and a system of ethics which were closely interrelated. For example, it is implausible that Keynes (or anyone else) would be a utilitarian in his ethics and an Aristotelian where probability is concerned.

The vertical lines in the diagram are self-evident because it is to be expected that a philosophy of probability would be reflected in Keynes's economics, and that a system of ethics might play a role in his political thought. It is also to be expected that Keynes's economics and politics might be complementary in some way. The diagonal relationships are less obvious but they too should be stressed. Keynes's ethics, which *inter alia* concerns the meaning of rationality, plays a role in his economics, and likewise his political thought was influenced by his probabilistic theory.

KEYNES AND PLATO

Since it is not possible to put much flesh on the skeleton in the course of this short paper I will confine myself to an account of his metaphysical outlook which slightly goes beyond *Keynes's Vision*. I have expressed Keynes's ideas in my own words and have not tried to provide textual evidence to support my interpretation.

Keynes's vision has been enigmatic and elusive for so long because it emanated from the fluid and rational spirituality that he described as a neo-Platonic religion. Keynes conceived it in his intellectual youth by developing particular Bloomsbury strands from the ideas of G.E. Moore. (Charles Hession has pointed out in correspondence that other Cambridge Apostles who became fervent Platonists include Lowes Dickinson and Lytton Strachey.)

The abstract Platonic insight which permeates Keynes's system is a strict division between the mental sphere of pure ideas and the real world of fluctuation and change. Long ago Plato accused the materialists of failing to appreciate the distance between ideas and the world, and Keynes's objection to the natural science of economics was that it invalidly tried to slur over that gap.

Like G.E. Moore, Keynes believed that universals originate and exist only in the mind; and although a concept may be chosen by reason and art to describe a collection of imperfectly similar units, nevertheless that concept cannot be assumed to exist in real life. He therefore drew a distinction – which is very much against the spirit of Ricardo and Walras – between a theory and the reality it is supposed to describe. Economics was a moral science because a judgement, based on moral and probabilistic knowledge, was necessary to intermediate between ideas and the world.

The Platonic metaphysics was conveyed with a poetical lyricism that Keynes did not try to imitate. Instead, he gave it a formal expression in the *Treatise on Probability* and it appears, in a gauche style but more obviously, in Keynes's early ethical writings. It manifested in the *Treatise* as the doctrine of rational intuition, which is the central theme of that work. According to the *Treatise* our state of knowledge of practical affairs is not sufficient, except in trivial instances such as structured games, to estimate the future prospects of events with quantitative precision. Nevertheless we can anticipate the future by seeing, in an artistic but rational way, that there is a pattern to the facts.

Because Platonists associate Being with both reason and goodness they do not consider that value judgements and facts can be differentiated in the modern way. Nor do they regard facts as the prerogative of reason while deprecating values as the product of an irrational emotion. They believe that all knowledge requires judgement, and that a judgement, whether it is of the positive or the normative variety, should be based on reason, operating within the context of understanding or intuition.

The notion that Keynes was a consequentialist, meaning a utilitarian, is based on a verbal confusion. I am aware that he wrote books and essays with the word 'consequences' in the title. Nevertheless, his world of elusive change is not consistent with utilitarianism, and Keynes criticized that doctrine repeatedly and without a word of qualification. Not only did the *Treatise on Probability* deny that there is any generally predictable connection between an action and its outcome; but even where the consequences were known, Keynes's ethics advocated, in the words of his early writings, 'being good' rather than 'doing good', for oneself or for others.

Keynes's Vision referred to this doctrine as a logic of motives rather than of consequences. Roy Weatherford has expressed the idea accurately and well:

> Keynes is using the word 'rational' to mean something much more like 'in accordance with the Laws of Thought' than like 'leading to success in practice' (Weatherford, 1982, p. 122).

Keynesian rationality means having the right reasons even if the answer is wrong. This does not imply – there is a semantic confusion to be avoided – that Keynes was never interested in the consequences of the policies he supported. It means that Keynes was not a consequentialist in the logical structure of his thought, but instead he formulated an idea of rationality which would be relevant in conditions of uncertainty, where the logic of rational economic man would not apply. Consequences usually (though not always) influenced the appropriateness of an action, and in this way determined whether the action should be performed.

The 'animal spirits' which appear in Keynes's theory of uncertainty are Platonic terminology for rational intuition, and refer to an implicit ideal against which the behaviour of investors is to be gauged. The account in Chapter 12 of the *General Theory* is that structural changes in the modern capital market had attracted speculators who had a short-term perspective but who were devoid of genuine insight into the productive possibilities of their investment. The (consequentialist) speculators were encouraged to estimate quantitatively the future of the market, even though their estimations had no rational foundation. When there was a sea change in economic conditions the rationale for the speculators' calculations disappeared. Investment became erratic and the economic system was destabilized through the investment multiplier.

The same Platonic metaphysics also permeates Keynes's political philosophy. In *Keynes's Vision* I highlighted a passing comment in which Keynes described himself as being 'on the extreme left wing of celestial space'. It meant that he began from classical philosophy, but wanted to jettison the way that philosophy had been applied. Although Keynes's policies were liberal, his political theory was drawn from an outlook typically associated with traditional conservation and the old Right. Far from being an unprincipled libertarian Keynes believed in duty; he accepted that there are moral categories, and he declared that 'no sane man can reasonably deny' the existence of evil.

In the eighteenth century, the enlightenment and the French Revolution discredited the metaphysical and spiritual philosophy which had long been perverted to justify the inequalities of the feudal system. We should regard Keynes's political philosophy as a reversion to a pre-enlightenment system of thought, intended to salvage his metaphysical ideals from the retrograde political system they had been used to defend. Keynes was not a liberal but a philosopher-king with a liberal orientation.

The irony is that, for so long, Keynes has been portrayed as a positivist who promoted the political and scientific neutrality of economics. Yet he was neither a positivist nor a socialist. He stood for the principle of a just and wisely managed economy, directed towards an ethical ideal 'with intellect and feelings in tune'.

THE IMPLICATIONS FOR KEYNESIANISM

It is only necessary to look at the unemployment figures over the decades to see the priceless gift, the theory of aggregate demand, which Keynes has given to the modern world. Yet the developed world has moved, probably for the good, closer to democratic values and further from the élitist moral and political structures which Keynes assumed. The moral and probabilistic insights which underlie his economics and politics are profound, and I believe, relevant and true; but these insights are often difficult to grasp and are easily perverted. Keynes's morals are contrary to the nihilistic spirit of our times and his political élitism could be dangerous in the wrong hands.

If it were not for his economic theory, it might be safer to say that Keynes's political economy, like the Platonic philosophy from which it ultimately derives, is based on an ideal which cannot be implemented in the real world. The difficulty is that Keynes's method, with all that it implies, is the only way we have of systematically thinking about the moving picture of economic experience. His doctrine is fascinating and controversial because it is perilous to ignore and perilous to adopt. He has formulated an economic and political philosophy which is dangerous for good or evil.

Bibliography

Aristotle (1908), *The Works*, W.D. Ross (ed.), Oxford: Clarendon Press.

Asimakopulos, A. (1988), 'The Aggregate Supply Function and the Share Economy' in O.F. Hamouda and J.N. Smithin (eds) *Keynes and Public Policy After Fifty Years*, vol. II, pp. 70–80.

Ayer, A.J. (1957), 'The Conception of Probability as a Logical Relation' in Korner, *Observation and Interpretation*.

Bateman, B.W. (1987), 'Keynes's Changing Conception of Probability', *Economics and Philosophy*, **3**, pp. 97–119.

Bateman, B.W. (1988), 'G.E. Moore and J.M. Keynes: A Missing Chapter in the History of the Expected Utility Model', *American Economic Review*, **78**, pp. 1098–106.

Bateman, B.W. (1989), '"Human Logic" and Keynes's Economics: A Comment', *Eastern Economic Journal*, **XV (1)**, pp. 63–67.

Bateman, B.W. (1990a), 'Keynes, Induction and Econometrics', *History of Political Economy*, **22**, pp. 359–79.

Bateman, B.W. (1990b), 'The Elusive Logical Relation', in Moggridge, *Perspectives in the History of Economic Thought.*

Boland, L.A. (1989), *The Methodology of Economic Model Building*, London: Routledge.

Brady, M.E. (1987), 'J.M. Keynes' "Theory of Evidential Weight": Its Relation to Information Processing Theory and Application in the *General Theory*', *Synthese*, **71**, pp. 37–59.

Braithwaite, R.B. (1946), 'Notes: John Maynard Keynes, First Baron Keynes of Tilton (1883–1946)', *Mind*, **55(219)**.

Braithwaite, R.B. (1973), 'Editorial Foreword' to *A Treatise on Probability*, Vol. VIII in D. Moggridge (ed.), *The Collected Writings of J.M. Keynes*, London: Macmillan.

Braithwaite, R.B. (1975), 'Keynes as Philosopher' in M. Keynes (ed.), *Essays on John Maynard Keynes*, Cambridge: Cambridge University Press.

'Britain's Industrial Future', being the Report of the Liberal Industrial Enquiry, (Ernest Benn, 1928).

Broad, C.D. (1914), *Perception, Physics and Reality*, Cambridge: Cambridge University Press.

Broad, C.D. (1922), 'Critical Notice on J.M. Keynes's *Treatise on Probability*', *Mind*, **31**.

Brothwell, J. (1988), 'The *General Theory* after Fifty Years – Why are We not all Keynesians now?' in J. Hillard (ed.), *J.M. Keynes in Retrospect*, pp. 45–63.

Brown-Collier, E. (1985), 'Keynes' View of an Organic Universe', *Review of Social Economy*, **13**, pp. 14–23.

Brown-Collier, E. and Bausor, R. (1988), 'The Epistemological Foundations of the *The General Theory*', *Scottish Journal of Political Economy*, **35(3)**, August, pp. 227–41.

Buckle, H. (1904), *History of Civilisation in England*, London: Henry Frowde.

Carabelli, A.M. (1982a), 'J.M. Keynes, "A Treatise on Probability"', in *Modelli di razionalitá nelle scienze economico-sociali* (Papers presented at the Conference on 'La razionalitá nelle scienze sociali', held in Modena, 9–11 October 1980), Arsenale, Venezia, pp. 115–37.

Carabelli, A.M. (1982b), 'On Keynes's Method: Practical Rationality', Cambridge, mimeo.

Carabelli, A.M. (1985), 'Keynes on Cause, Chance and Possibility', in Lawson and Pesaran, *Keynes' Economics*, pp. 151–80.

Carabelli, A.M. (1987), '"Il solo socialista presente": Keynes e i laburisti', *Il Ponte*, **42(6)**, pp. 179–90.

Carabelli, A.M. (1988), *On Keynes's Method*, London: Macmillan.

Chick, V. (1985), 'Time and the Wage-unit in the Method of *The General Theory*: History and Equilibrium' in Lawson and Pesaran (eds) *Keynes's Economics*, pp. 195–205.

Clarke, P. (1989), *The Keynesian Revolution in the Making: 1924–1936*, Oxford: Oxford University Press.

Coddington, A. (1983), *Keynesian Economics – The Search for First Principles*, London: Allen and Unwin.

Cohen, L.J. (1977), *The Probable and The Provable*, Oxford: Oxford University Press.

Cohen, L.J. (1985), 'Twelve Questions about Keynes's Concept of Weight', *British Journal for the Philosophy of Science*, **37**.

Davis, J.B. (1989), 'Keynes on Atomism and Organicism', *Economic Journal*, **99**, pp. 1159–72.

Davis, J.B. (1989–90), 'Keynes and Organicism: Comment', *Journal of Post Keynesian Economics*, **12(2)**, pp. 308–15.

Davis, J.B. (1991), 'Keynes's Critiques of Moore', *Cambridge Journal of Economics*, forthcoming.

Dow, S.C. (1988), 'What Happened to Keynes's Economics?' in O.F. Hamouda and J.N. Smithin (eds), *Keynes and Public Policy After Fifty Years*, vol. I, pp. 101–11.

Evans, P., Skocpol, T. and Rueschemeyer, D. (eds) (1985), *Bringing the State Back In*, Cambridge: Cambridge University Press.

Favereau, O. (1985), 'L'incertain dans la "révolution Kéynesienne". L'hypothèse Wittgenstein', *Economies et Sociétés*, (3), pp. 29–72.

Fitzgibbons, A. (1988), *Keynes's Vision: A New Political Economy*, Oxford: Clarendon Press.

Freeman, M. (1980), *Edmund Burke and the Critique of Political Radicalism*, Oxford: Basil Blackwell.

Good, I.J. (1950), *Probability in the Weighing of Evidence*, Charles Griffin.

Gottinger, H.H. (1983), *Coping with Complexity. Perspectives for Economics, Management and Social Sciences*, Dordrecht: Reidel.

Gourevitch, P.A. (1989), 'Keynesian Politics: The Political Sources of Economic Policy Choices', in Hall (ed.), *The Political Power of Economic Ideas*.

Greenstein, C.H. (1978), *Dictionary of Logical Terms and Symbols*, New York: Van Nostrand Reinhold.

Grunberg, E. (1966), 'The Meaning and Scope of External Boundaries in Economics' in S.R. Krupp (ed.), *The Structure of Economic Science*, Englewood Cliffs, NJ: Prentice-Hall, pp. 148–65.

Grunberg, E. (1978), '"Complexity" and "Open Systems" in Economic Discourse', *Journal of Economic Issues*, **12**(3), September, pp. 541–60.

Hacking, J. (1983), *Representing and Intervening*, New York: Cambridge University Press.

Hall, P.A. (ed.) (1989), *The Political Power of Economic Ideas*, Princeton: Princeton University Press.

Hamouda, O. and Smithin, J. (1988a), 'Some remarks on "Uncertainty and economic analysis"', *Economic Journal*, **98**, pp. 159–64.

Hamouda, O.F. and Smithin, J.N. (eds) (1988b), *Keynes and Public Policy After Fifty Years. Volume I: Economics and Policy. Volume II: Theories and Method*, Aldershot: Edward Elgar.

Harrod, R.F. (1938), 'Scope and Method of Economics', *Economic Journal*, **48**, pp. 383–402.

Harrod, R.F. (1974), *Foundations of Inductive Logic*, London: Macmillan.

Harrod, R.F. (1951), *The Life of John Maynard Keynes*, London:

Macmillan.

Hayek, A. (1978), *New Studies in Philosophy, Politics and Economics*, London: Routledge and Kegan.

Hession, C. (1984), *John Maynard Keynes: A Personal Biography*, New York: Macmillan.

Hamblin, C.L. (1970), *Fallacies*, London: Methuen.

Hillard, J. (ed.) (1988), *J.M. Keynes in Retrospect. The Legacy of the Keynesian Revolution*, Aldershot: Edward Elgar.

Hilpinen, R. (1970), 'On the Information Provided by Observations' in Hintikka and Suppes, *Aspects of Inductive Logic*.

Hintikka, J. and Suppes, P. (eds) (1966), *Aspects of Inductive Logic*, New York: North-Holland.

Howson, S. and Winch, D. (1977), *The Economic Advisory Council 1930–39*, Cambridge, Cambridge University Press.

Hutchison, T.W. (1981), *The Politics and Philosophy of Economics: Marxians, Keynesians and Austrians*, Oxford: Basil Blackwell.

Kahn, R.F. (1984), *The Making of Keynes's General Theory*, Cambridge: Cambridge University Press.

Keynes, J.M. (1904–1910), unpublished writings, Cambridge: King's College, Cambridge University:

(1904a), 'Ethics in Relation to Conduct'

(1904b), 'The Greatest of These'

(1904c), The Political Doctrines of Edmund Burke'

(1905a), 'Toleration'

(1905b), 'Modern Civilization'

(1905c), 'A Theory of Beauty'

(1906), 'Egoism'

(1910), untitled essay arguing on the intrinsic moral value of complex human character traits

(nd), 'Have We a Panacea?'

Keynes, J.M. (1907), 'The Principles of Probability', first dissertation.

Keynes, J.M. (1908), 'The Principles of Probability', second dissertation.

Keynes, J.M. (1973–89), *The Collected Writings of Maynard Keynes*, Vols I–XXX, D.E. Moggridge and E. Johnson (eds), London: Macmillan.

I   *Indian Currency and Finance*

II   *The Economic Consequences of the Peace*

III   *A Revision of the Treaty*

IV   *A Tract on Monetary Reform*

V   *A Treatise on Money, 1 The Pure Theory of Money*

VI   *A Treatise on Money, 2 The Applied Theory of Money*

VII	*The General Theory of Employment, Interest and Money*
VIII	*Treatise on Probability*
IX	*Essays in Persuasion*
X	*Essays in Biography*
XI	*Economic Articles and Correspondence: Academic*
XII	*Economic Articles and Correspondence: Investment and Editorial*
XIII	*The General Theory and After: Part I, Preparation*
XIV	*The General Theory and After: Part II, Defence and Development*
XV	*Activities 1906–14: India and Cambridge*
XVI	*Activities 1914–19: The Treasury and Versailles*
XVII	*Activities 1920–2: Treaty Revision and Reconstruction*
XVIII	*Activities 1922–32: The End of Reparations*
XIX	*Activities 1922–9: 2 Vols., The Return to Gold and Industrial Policy, I and II*
XX	*Activities 1929–31: Rethinking Employment and Unemployment Policies*
XXI	*Activities 1931–9: World Crises and Policies in Britain and America*
XXII	*Activities 1939–45: Internal War Finance*
XXIII	*Activities 1940–3: External War Finance*
XXIV	*Activities 1944–6: The Transition to Peace*
XXV	*Activities 1940–4: Shaping the Post-War World: The Clearing Union*
XXVI	*Activities 1941–6: Shaping the Post-War World: Bretton Woods and Reparation*
XXVII	*Activities 1940–6: Shaping the Post-War World: Employment and Commodities*
XXVIII	*Social, Political and Literary Writings*
XXIX	*The General Theory and After: A Supplement*
XXX	*Bibliography and Index.*

Keynes, J.N. (1955), *The Scope and Method of Political Economy*, New York: Kelley and Millman.

Kilmanock, A. (ed.) (1987), *The Radical Challenge*, London: Deutsch Publications.

Korner, S. (ed.) (1957), *Observation and Interpretation*, New York: Butterworths.

Kramnick, I. (1977), *The Rage of Edmund Burke: Portrait of an Ambivalent Conservative*, New York: Basic Books.

Lakatos, I. (1968a), 'Changes in the Problem of Inductive Logic' in Lakatos, *The Problem of Inductive Logic*.

Lakatos, I. (1968b), *The Problem of Inductive Logic*, North-Holland.

Lawson, T. (1985), 'Uncertainty and Economic Analysis', *Economic Journal*, **95**, December, pp. 909–27.

Lawson, T. (1987), 'The Relative/Absolute Nature of Knowledge and Economic Analysis', *Economic Journal*, **97**, December, pp. 951–70.

Lawson, T. (1989), 'Realism and Instrumentalism in the Development of Econometrics', *Oxford Economic Papers*, **41(1)**, January, pp. 236–58.

Lawson, T. and Pesaran, H. (eds) (1985), *Keynes' Economics. Methodological Issues* (Papers presented at the Conference on 'Methodological Issues in Keynesian Economics', Trinity College, Cambridge, 12–14 September 1983), London: Croom Helm.

Lecky, W. (1891), *A History of England in the Eighteenth Century*.

Levi, I. (1973), *Gambling with Truth*, Cambridge, MA: MIT Press.

McQueen, D. (1988), 'The Hidden Microeconomics of J.M. Keynes' in O.F. Hamouda and J.N. Smithin (eds), *Keynes and Public Policy After Fifty Years*, vol. I.

Malthus, T.R. (1986), *The Works*, E.A. Wrigley and D. Souden (eds), London: Pickering and Chatto.

Meltzer, A.H. (1989), *Keynes's Monetary Thought*. Cambridge: Cambridge University Press.

Moggridge, D.E. (1988), 'The Keynesian Revolution in Historical Perspective' in O.F. Hamouda and J.N. Smithin (eds), *Keynes and Public Policy After Fifty Years*, vol. I.

Moggridge, D.E. (ed.), (1990), '*Perspectives on the History of Economic Thought*, vols. 3 and 4, Aldershot: Edward Elgar.

Moggridge, D.E. and Howson, S.K. (1974), 'Keynes on Monetary Policy, 1910–1946', *Oxford Economic Papers*, **26**, pp. 226–47.

Mongin, Ph. (1988), 'Le réalism des hypothèses et la *Partial Interpretation View*', *Philosophy of Social Science*, **18**, pp. 281–325.

Moore, G.E. (1903), *Principia Ethica*, Cambridge: Cambridge University Press.

Moore, G.E. (1912), *Ethics*, Oxford: Oxford University Press.

Morgenbesser, S. (1969), 'The Realist–Instrumentalist Controversy', in Morgenbesser, Suppe and White (eds), *Philosophy, Science and Method*, New York: St. Martin Press, pp. 200–18.

Morin, E. (1977–86), *La Méthode. I. La Nature de la Nature (1977): La Méthode. II. La Vie de la Vie (1980): La Méthode. III La Connaissance de la Connaissance (1986)*, Paris: Le Seuil.

Morin, E. (1984), 'Epistemologie de la complexité' in C. Atias and J.L. Le Moigne (eds), *Edgar Morin. Science et conscience de la complexité*, Aix-en-Provence: Librairie de l'Université.

Morin, E. (1985), 'Le vie della complessitá' in G. Bocchi and M. Ceruti (eds), *La sfida della complessitá*, Milan: Feltrinelli, pp. 49–60.

Morley, J. (1867), *Edmund Burke: A Historical Study*, London: Macmillan.

Morley, J. (1879), *Burke*, New York: Harper and Brothers.

Nagel, E. (1963), 'Assumptions in Economic Theory', *American Economic Review, Papers and Proceedings*, May, pp. 211–19.

Nicolis, G. (1986), 'Dissipative Systems', *Reports on Progress in Physics*, **49**, pp. 873–949.

O'Donnell, R. (1982), *Keynes: Philosophy and Economics. An Approach to Rationality and Uncertainty*, Ph D dissertation, Cambridge (GB).

O'Donnell, R.M. (1989a), *Keynes: Philosophy, Economics and Politics: The Philosophical Foundations of Keynes's Thought and their Influence on His Economics and Politics*, London: Macmillan.

O'Donnell, R.M. (1989b), 'Keynes Weight of Argument and Popper's Paradox', unpublished manuscript.

O'Donnell, R.M. (1990), 'Continuity in Keynes's Conception of Probability', in D.E. Moggridge (ed.), *Perspectives on the History of Economic Thought*, **4**, Aldershot, Edward Elgar.

Parkin, C. (1956), *The Moral Basis of Burke's Political Thought*, New York: Russell & Russell.

Parsons, D.W. (1985), 'Was Keynes Kuhnian? Keynes and the Idea of Theoretical Revolutions', *British Journal of Political Science*, **15**, October, pp. 451–71.

Peden, G.C. (1988), *Keynes, The Treasury, and British Economic Policy*, London: Macmillan.

Peirce, C.S. (1965), *The Collected Papers of Charles Sanders Peirce*, C. Hartshorne and P. Weiss (eds), Cambridge: Harvard University Press.

Pocock, J.G.A. (1985), *Virtue, Commerce, and History: Essays on Political Thought and History, Chiefly in the Eighteenth Century*, Cambridge: Cambridge University Press.

Popper, K.R. (1972), *The Logic of Scientific Discovery*, London: Hutchinson.

Popper, K.R. (1983), *Realism and the Aim of Science*, London: Hutchinson.

Prigogine, I. (1980), *From Being to Becoming*, San Francisco: Freeman.

Prigogine, I. and Nicolis, G. (1986), *Mastering Complexity*, Munich: Piper.

Prigogine, I. and Stengers, I. (1981), ' Semplice/Complesso' in *Enciclopedia Einaudi*, Turin: Einaudi.

Putnam, H. (1981), *Reason, Truth and History*, Cambridge: Cambridge University Press.

Ramsey, F.P. (1931), *Foundations of Mathematics*, London: Routledge and Kegan Paul.

Raphael, D.D. (1974), 'Sidgwick on Intuitionism', *Monist*.

Rawls, J. (1955), 'Two Concepts of Rules', *Philosophical Review*, 64, pp. 3–32.

Rawls, J. (1971), *A Theory of Justice*, Cambridge, MA: Harvard University Press.

Robbins, L. (1936), *An Essay on the Nature and Significance of Economic Science*, (2nd edn), London: Macmillan.

Robbins, L. (1938), 'Interpersonal Comparisons of Utility: A Comment', *Economic Journal*, 48, pp. 635–41.

Robinson, J. (1962), *Economic Philosophy*, Chicago: Aldine.

Rotheim, R.J. (1981), 'Keynes's Monetary Theory of Value (1933), *Journal of Post Keynesian Economics*, 3(4), Summer, pp. 568–85.

Russell, B. (1967), *Autobiography of Bertrand Russell: 1872–1914*, London: George Allen & Unwin.

Schneewind, J.B. (1977), *Sidgwick's Ethics and Victorian Moral Philosophy*, Oxford: Clarendon Press.

Shapere, D. (1982), 'The Concept of Observation in Science and Philosophy', *Philosophy of Science*, 49, pp. 485–525.

Sidgwick, H. (1907), *The Methods of Ethics*, (7th edn), London: Macmillan.

Simon, H. (1962), 'The Architecture of Complexity', *American Philosophical Society, Proceedings*, 106, April, pp. 467–82.

Skidelsky, R. (1983), *John Maynard Keynes, Vol. I, Hopes Betrayed, 1883–1920*, London: Macmillan.

Skidelsky, R. (1987), 'Keynes's Political Legacy', in A. Kilmanock (ed.), *The Radical Challenge*, London: Deutsch Publications.

Stanlis, P.J. (1958), *Edmund Burke and Natural Law*, Ann Arbor: University of Michigan Press.

Stohs, M. (1980), '"Uncertainty" in Keynes's *General Theory*', *History of Political Economy*, 12(3).

Stone, R. (1978), 'Keynes, Political Arithmetic and Econometrics', *Proceedings of the British Academy*, LXIV, Oxford: Oxford University Press.

Surrey, M. (1988), 'The Great Recession 1974–84: Is a "Keynesist" Approach Plausible?' in J. Hillard (ed.) *J.M. Keynes in Retrospect*, pp. 107–24.

Urmson, J.O. (1970), 'Moore's Utilitarianism', in A. Ambrose and M. Lazerwitz (eds), *G.E. Moore: Essays in Retrospect*, London: George Allen & Unwin.

Walker, D.A. (1985), 'Keynes as a Historian of Economic Thought: the Biographical Essays on Neoclassical Economists', *History of Political Economy*, **17(2)**, pp. 159–86.

Weatherford, R. (1982), *Philosophical Foundations of Probability Theory*, London: Routledge and Kegan Paul.

Weeks, J. (1988), 'Value and Production in *The General Theory*' in J. Hillard (ed.), *J.M. Keynes in Retrospect*, pp. 185–210.

Weir, M. (1990), 'Ideas and Politics: The Acceptance of Keynesianism in Britain and the United States' in Hall (ed.), *The Political Power of Economic Ideas*.

Weir, M. and Skocpol, T. (1985), 'State Structures and the Possibilities for "Keynesian" Responses to the Great Depression in Sweden, Britain and the United States' in Evans *et. al.*, *Bringing the State Back In*.

Weintraub, E.R. (1975), 'Uncertainty and the Keynesian Revolution', *History of Political Economy*, **7**, pp. 730–45.

Wells, P. (1986), '"Mr Churchill" and the *The General Theory*', in J.S. Cohen and G.C. Harcourt (eds), *International Monetary Problems and Supply-Side Economics*, London: Macmillan, pp. 8–27.

Wilkins, Burleigh Taylor (1967), *The Problem of Burke's Political Philosophy*, Oxford: Clarendon Press.

Winslow, E.G. (1986), '"Human Logic" and Keynes's Economics', *Eastern Economic Journal*, **12**, October–December, pp. 413–30.

Winslow, E.G. (1989), 'Organic Interdependence, Uncertainty and Economic Analysis', *Economic Journal*, **99**, pp. 1173–82.

Index